AF553412

Politics and Religion

Politics and Religion

Edited by
Saitya Brata Das

POLITICS AND RELIGION
Edited by Saitya Brata Das

First Published, 2014

ISBN 978-93-5002-307-5

Published by
AAKAR BOOKS
28 E Pocket IV, Mayur Vihar Phase I, Delhi 110 091
Phone : 011 2279 5505 Telefax : 011 2279 5641
info@aakarbooks.com; www.aakarbooks.com

Printed at
Saurabh Printers Pvt. Ltd., A 16, Sector IV, Noida

Price: ₹ 495

Contents

Acknowledgements

The publication of this book financially benefits from the University Grants Commission under the Special Assistance Programme that is granted to Centre for English Studies of Jawaharlal Nehru University. I wish to thank my colleagues at the Centre for English Studies (CES) for making this possible. I thank Mr. K.K. Saxena of Aakar Books for bringing out this book in a short time. "Thanks" goes to students and research scholars of CES for making the conference on *Politics and Religion* a big success and this volume is a collection of the papers presented at that conference—such an unforgettable event. The editor of this volume, who was also the coordinator of the conference, wishes to thank Mohinder Singh and Rajarshi Dasgupta from Jawaharlal Nehru University and Prasanta Chakravarty from Delhi University for making the conference such an enriching experience for all of us.

April 2014 **Saitya Brata Das**

Contributors

Achia Anzi teaches Hebrew at the School of Language, Literature and Culture Studies at Jawaharlal Nehru University, Delhi.

Soumyabrata Choudhury currently teaches at the School of Arts and Aesthetics, Jawaharlal Nehru University, Delhi. He has previously taught at CSSSC. Kolkata, and has been a fellow at Centre for Studies of Developing Societies, Delhi and Indian Institute of Advanced Study, Shimla. His book *Theatre, Number, Event: Three Studies on the Relationship of Sovereignty, Power and Truth* was published by IIAS, Shimla in 2013.

Clayton Crockett is Professor and Director of Religious Studies at the University of Central Arkansas. He is the author of *Deleuze Beyond Badiou* and *Religion, Politics, and the Earth* (with Jeffrey W. Robbins). Crockett is also a co-editor of the book series "Insurrections: Critical Studies in Religion, Politics, and Culture" with Columbia University Press.

Saitya Brata Das was a Fellow at Indian Institute of Advanced Study, Shimla from 2009 to 2011. Currently he is Associate Professor at Centre for English Studies, Jawaharlal Nehru University. He is associated with the UFR Philosophie, Université de Strasbourg, France, and with *Maison des Sciences de L'Homme*, Paris, where he was Post Doctorate fellow during the academic year 2006-2007. His first book length study called *The Promise of Time: Towards a Phenomenology of Promise* is published from Indian Institute of Advanced Study, India.

Soumick De is pursuing his PhD at Centre for Theatre and Performance Studies, School of Arts and Aesthetics, Jawaharlal Nehru University, New Delhi. His essay titled *Law, Reason, Truth: Three Paradigmatic Problems Concerning Truth* has been published in *Kritike*, (December 2013). Soumick is currently working on his doctoral thesis titled *Perversion, Pedagogy and the Comic: A Survey of the Concept of Theatre in the Christian Middle Ages.*

Harjeet Singh Gill, a renowned semiotician and thinker, is Professor Emeritus of Jawaharlal Nehru University. Some of his recent publications are: *Baba Nanak, Sufi Rhythms: Interpreted in Free Verse,* and *Conceptualism in Buddhist and French Traditions*. The last mentioned work is the revised edition of his lectures in College de France, Paris, as a Visiting Professor in 1998.

Franson Manjali serves as Professor of Linguistics and Semiotics at Jawaharlal Nehru University (JNU), New Delhi. After being awarded doctorate at JNU in 1986, he taught for a year at University of Delhi, and then went on to pursue two years of post-doctoral studies in Paris (Paris-4, Sorbonne, and L'Ecole des Hautes Etudes En Sciences Sociales) where he wrote a monograph *Nuclear Semantics: Towards a Theory of Relational Meaning* (Bahri, 1991). He joined the JNU faculty in October 1989. During 1998-99, he had a stint as a Fellow at Indian Institute of Advanced Study (IIAS) during which his intellectual orientation veered from Semiotics and Cognitive Science towards the Poststructuralist philosophies. His book, *Literature and Inûnity* (2001), published by IIAS, Shimla, attests to this shift, and contains texts relating to the works of Lévinas, Blanchot, Derrida and Nancy. His more recent publications *Language, Discourse and Culture: Contemporary Philosophical Perspectives* (Anthem, 2007) and *Labyrinths of Language: Philosophical Investigations* (Aakar Books, 2014) contain essays that explore and analyse issues in language studies, literature, culture and philosophy from the post-structuralist and postcolonial viewpoints.

Dhananjay Singh is Assistant Professor at Centre for English Studies, Jawaharlal Nehru University, New Delhi, where he teaches courses and supervises research in Indian aesthetics, comparative aesthetics, Indian philosophy of language, creative writing, Irish literature, nineteenth century literature, and poetry. Dhananjay is also Assistant Editor, *Encyclopedia of Indian Poetics*, a project of Sahitya Akademi, New Delhi, sponsored by UNESCO. He is the author of *Fables in the Indian Narrative Tradition* (2011), and has contributed articles in the areas of Indian aesthetics, philosophy of language, comparative poetics, and Indian literature.

Milind Wakankar's 2010 work, *Subalternity and Religion*, tries to bring together texts of medieval Indian mystic thought on the one hand, and the works of Schelling, Rosenzweig, Heidegger and Levinas on the other. He is now writing about the the work of fluency in the Indo-Islamic millennium, taking his cues from the late Heidegger on language. He teaches at Indian Institute of Technology, Delhi.

Introduction: Thinking without Sovereignty

Saitya Brata Das

I

The "crisis" of liberal democracies in today's world demands from us re-investigation of the notion of the "political". Since the dominant notion of the "political" that is associated with the liberal-democratic assignment of its significance is at its fundamental level inseparable from certain determination of secularization as historical reason, with the crisis of liberal democracies and concomitantly with the exhaustion of the notion of "secularization", the problem of religion/ theological has come to assume profound significance for us once more. Hence is the demand to re-think the notion of the "political" in relation to the "theological", a relation that is enigmatic insofar as this relation has never ceased to haunt the stakes of our historical existence. Does such a demand to re-think religion or theological (here we are using these two terms interchangeably) in its relation to the political merit, the saying, which often appears convenient to us, a saying that is at the same time extremely strenuous and difficult to utter: "return of religion"?

Thus in recent politico-philosophical discourses, discourses that are rigorously attentive to such historical transformations of our condition, we hear the saying: "return of religion". In what sense is there a "re-turn" of religion? To put a question in an even more preliminary mode and therefore is all the more necessary to ask: what does *re-turn* mean in this "re-turn" of "religion"? What are the senses of the term "re-ligion" that may (not) have a lot to do with the sense of "re-turn" itself? We may wonder whether the very essence of religion itself has something essential to do with the sense of "re-turn" (one of the meanings of "re-ligion" that we know is "re-linking" or "re-binding" or even "re-turning"). One may thus further ponder: does not the sense of "religion" itself invite us to think of "returning" in the manner that the essence of religion itself is determined thereupon as "return". Is the promise or danger of religion exhausted in this sense of "re-turn" (whereto?) to/of something that is autochthonous and originary, a movement of turning back to an arché-originary moment? Or rather the more essential promise of religion is to be found elsewhere, not so much in the retrieval of a given past that is congealed in a closed tradition despite some centuries of "secularization" process, but rather that has to do with a true eschatological sense of religion where *eschaton* has not so much to do with the concept of the end of the world (as it is generally understood), but rather that of *opening of the world* that infinitely affirms the arriving and *coming to presence*, the future that must be hoped against all hopelessness. Religion, in this eschatological sense, has something essential thing to do with hope, a radical hope that *ad-ventures* beyond all hoped-for. Religion will thus be considered as this *ad-venture* of hope, as a messianic opening of the world from the iron cages of oppression. Thus Ernst Bloch, the atheistic messianic thinker of religion, could say that where there is hope, must there be also religion, for what ties religion to hope—in their innermost ground—is this eschatological affirmation of what "not yet" (*Noch Nicht*).

At stake here is the notion of the "political" itself. In what manner and by what measure should we be able to *differentiate*, if at all should we differentiate, between the *differential* senses of religion in relation to the political? It appears as if the future task of thinking lies in this intensification of difference between a certain determination of politics as the politics of the originary, a return of autochthony that has never ceased to deploy religion for legitimacy of earthly sovereignties, and on the other hand, the eschatological affirmation, beyond any positivistic or negativistic terms, of the future as its fundamental *attunement* of hope? As we see that in both senses of the political it is the sense of the theological that is at stake. There is a theo-politics that has never been able to establish its sense without simultaneously establishing the theological, and there is the other theological that insists in the interruption of the political, *deferring* and *differing* the political and thus opening of the space wherein any and each principle of sovereignties is de-legitimated. In both cases it is essentially the problem of "re-turn": the (im)possibility of the "return of religion" without simultaneous disruption of the political, return of religion that returns by disrupting the mythic autochthony of the same.

Anyone who wants to think today on the (non)relation of religion with the political can't escape the experience of this interval or this spacing that unites or separates this "re-turn", making "return" never a simple affair without a simultaneous exposing us to a desert or wilderness. At the heart of this agonal spacing of the political and theological lies the unconditional claim of the ethical justice which must be salvaged ever anew as the redemptive possibility to come, messianic in the verbality of its resonance, from this very *agon.* In that sense, the notion of justice bears an ethical sense in-excess over the political; as if there is no politics without being abandoned to such a desert of justice to come.

This unconditional claim of justice renders the return of religion at once possible and even necessary on the one hand, and impossible and dangerous at the same time. This is precisely what messianism always insists upon: the true affirmation of future, that is affirmation of justice to come, is always an experience of the interval that never allows it to be closed once and for all. Whenever this interval or this spacing is sought to be closed, unspeakable evil bursts forth and all hell lets itself loose on earth. Therefore messianism always insists, in the name of the unconditional justice, on the necessity and the demand of de-legitimization of sovereignties. As though the ethical insistence on the unconditional justice to come must pass through a thinking without sovereignties. If there is any sense of religion for messianism—and in a very fundamental sense messianism bears a "religious" sense—it is in this sense of "religion" that does not allow itself to serve as legitimizing the foundation of sovereignty. If we understand "political" as the process of legitimization, as a realm where conditioned negotiations take place between given "forces" or "powers", then messianism wrests the question of justice from the domain of the political and simultaneously subjecting religion itself to deconstruction, enabling thereby the affirmative dimension of religion to emerge which is the true eschatological and messianic opening of *justice to come* in hope. Hope is thus fundamental to religion, in all religion, in such a manner that it permits us to deconstruct religion itself. It is in this sense there is perhaps a "return of religion". It is the characteristic of hope always to return, but it is never a return of religion in the sense of returning of the autochthonous or the originary to legitimize worldly power on the ground of the political, but as the never ceasing returning of hope and affirmation of justice *to come.* Secularism as a historical critique is therefore not abandoned but its exhaustion is put to work once again and is radicalized beyond its reduction into the world-historical conformism and into the legitimization of worldly-political powers that secretly never ceased to use religion as its hidden weapon. Similarly the return of religion is not abandoned in the name of a facile materialism, opportunistic secularism or even a naive atheism but its promise is rescued and affirmed in the very name of its unconditional justice from its abuse to legitimize world-historical powers. Such abuse of religion by the world historical-political powers to legitimize its domination is to be found all over our historical world across countries and times, whether it is East or West, through irreducibly different historical forms. It will thus be a very interesting task to undertake historical investigations into the theological-political nexus in different historical times and places so as to formulate a different concept of the political and a more radical concept of the theological for our time. Such investigations are underway in many parts of today's world.

II

To re-think religion today at this epochal closure of metaphysics (as Heidegger says) of which the crisis of secular liberal politics is one of the most visible characteristics, is to think re-ligion, in a fundamental manner, as de-legitimation. If such a metaphysics is constituted as "onto-theologically", then re-thinking religion outside metaphysics must exceed both "theological" (in the sense of "theo" as the permanent ground of beings; "theo" as ground) and "a-theological" (in the sense that a certain thought structure called "liberalism", coming from the Enlightenment, calls it "secular"); as if, as it were, religion can't be exhausted in these already given, now stale and banal, determinations like "theological" or "atheistic". At the beginning of the 20th century Walter Benjamin grasped this necessity to re-think religion without sovereignty and without legitimization as that which disrupts the mythic continuum of a historical Reason. In that sense, modernity's claim, which it inherits from the Enlightenment's legacy by historicizing Reason, that it has successfully replaced the mythic order of the world by the historical—is profoundly mistaken. Far from Reason being incommensurable to myth, Reason rather mythologizes the historical. Religion is, then, reduced to the mythic so as to be conjured it away, and yet, at the same time, can be secretly used up as a puppet through which the dominant power, in the name of this "historical Reason", is to win all the time. As against the abuse of religion by the dominant power of earthly sovereignties, Benjamin evokes the religion of messianism by disjoining religion from the mythic foundation of legitimacy and legality. If the essence of law has a mythic foundation and if the dominant political power in the earthly order legitimizes its *raison d'etat* through constant acts of legitimization by law-positing and law-preserving violence, then religion for Benjamin opens up to a divine violence outside law which is not founded by myth in turn. Such divine violence is, paradoxically, without violence, for it redeems all violence. What messianism opens to is this restitution of immortality, which is redemptive, through an infinite suspension of law. Between the passing of judgment on one hand, and on the other, the infinite deferral of its execution lies a yawning abyss in which justice arrives. This makes justice forever incommensurable to law. It is this incommensurability, opened by religion that is the task of thinking today as against the mythic continuum of beings, against the law-posited and law-preserved continuity of historical Reason. Benjamin attempts to think such messianic justice as the only way in which past oppressions and sufferings of the oppressed and the vanquished can be redeemed. For that to happen, we must learn to bring that radical disjunction into the heart of the world between the messianic-religious claim of justice and the political pursuit of happiness in the profane order.

Here Benjamin is putting the stakes of his faith elsewhere than in the secular-liberal pursuit of happiness through infinite pragmatic negotiations of conditioned "rights", for such "rights" even to be possible, there must *always already* be opening up of the possibility of justice that is incommensurable to law. This "always already" is the promise before the law. Without such promise, the infinite acts of the establishment of conditional rights through pragmatic negotiations will end up in the mythic recurrence of violence where the exceptional violence of law-positing turns into routine violence. That through such infinite pragmatic negotiations, where law is the means, the unconditional justice is sure to be established: this is the myth of the secular-liberal democracies. It tacitly presupposes a commensuration which, by definition, justice suspends. Hence religion, in a profounder sense, has always been a scandal for the metaphysical essence of such politics. Instead of opening up the political to such scandalous religion of unconditional justice, it rather grounds political itself on the theological-mythic foundation.

If there is a "re-turn" of religion today, it must be considered as return of a scandal that makes impossible the worldly immanence of self-presence. As de-legitimization of all worldly sovereign powers, the scandal of religion keeps alive the other absolute demand of mankind for unconditional happiness or justice. It is thus an absolute hope contra all hopelessness of the world. But this hope against all worldly hopelessness is not in turn the "other" world of hope against "this" world of hopeless, but otherwise than the world at all. Religion is "un-worldly" in that sense and not "other-worldly": happiness is not realized in this "worldly" world, nor in that another world beyond, but which, in its arrival, calls into question each worldly world in the name of the world *to come*. In welcome the otherwise than the worldly into the heart of the world is the aporia wherein hinges and unhinges what we call "ethics" and "politics" today.

III

This edited volume of essays is a collection of papers presented at a conference on *Politics and/of Religion* organized at Jawaharlal Nehru University in November 2013. The papers by Clayton Crockett and Franson Manjali are the exceptions here; they are especially invited for this collection. Though each essay is singular and different in its orientation, and each in its own manner approaches the question of politics and religion in today's world, nevertheless the reader—so it is hoped—will discover surprising affinities among them. The editor, thus, resists himself the temptation to exhibit a homogeneous, unifying thesis underlying these papers which are written from different perspectives and have different concerns. There is not only one single question that is being posed in these essays, and not only one answer is being provided. Far from being a weakness, the editor thinks that it rather constitutes the strength of this collection. Nevertheless what appears to be interesting here, as it is bound to be, is this bringing together —without reducing them into a unifying thesis—of each time singular attempt to think the same, that is, the very complicated (non)relation between politics and/of religion. In that sense, this conjunction "and" that brings together politics and religion, is haunted by an unnamed disjunction that *sets apart* politics and religion. Similarly the title of the conference— *Politics and/of Religion*—can also be read as Politics *of* Religion in which haunts—in the place "of"—a "without": Politics *without* Religion. We may also reverse it into : Religion *without* Politics. In each case there is a spectre of difference haunting each of our attempts to constitutes certain unity of form of which difference could be understood only as an attenuated difference of a more primordial identity.

This complexity of the title is reduced in the simplified title of this volume, which is now read simply as: *Politics and Religion*. However, the reader is invited to reflect on the (non)relation of politics and religion as it is sought to be heard in the original title of the conference.

The first paper of this collection, Clayton Crockett's *Political Theology without Sovereignty: Reading Derrida Reading Religion* touches the very heart of this question of the relation of the political and theological. Reading some of the later works by Jacques Derrida, Crockett attempts to see the possibility of a political theology emerging in Derrida's later works, a political theology that has less to do with the notion of exception constituting the monothetic and nomothetic operation of a sovereign figure, but more to do with the exceptionality of a messianic justice always in excess of law that defers and differs its actualization in the political realm of conditioned negotiations and pragmatic resolutions. Derrida's works, thus, can be said to have a certain proximity with the politico-theological reflections of Walter Benjamin and Emmanuel Lévinas. Whether in proximity with Benjamin (that is, in his thinking of justice in excess of law) and in proximity with Emmanuel Lévinas (that is, in his thinking of ethical in excess of politics), there is his attempt to think of an excess which is also an impoverishment, that which —being excessive and impoverished at the same time—does not assume the force of law in turn. Crockett shows in this essay, as elsewhere, that such political theology, if this name can at all be retained to think with Derrida (Crockett suggests that it is indeed possible), such political theology must be heterogeneous to the logic of exception as it found expression in Carl Schmitt's political theology, wherein the exception to law—precisely by being an exception—serves the re-institution of legitimacy of the given order of law. My own essay follows somewhat the same line of argument. Reading Friedrich Joseph von Schelling's early works, I try to argue that in Schellingian eschatology there is to be found a radical political theology that radically puts into question the attempts to legitimize worldly political sovereignties on a theological foundation. Unlike Hegel, Schelling thus sees the figure of the modern state less as a figure of the absolute but rather as mankind's impoverished attempt to supplement a fundamental void, marked by the event of the Fall, and which, as such, is destined to pass away. The worldly sovereignties thereby lose their claim of ultimate normative obligation from us. Schelling saw in the eschatological essence of religion a caesura, a hiatus, a difference between the political and theological in such a way that religion is seen as that which sets the world apart from its foundation, keeping the world thereby open to what is to come, the unground and ungroundable holy.

In his thoughtful essay *Truth and Reason in Religion and Politics,* Harjeet Singh Gill ruminates on the dialectical relationship between the universal claims of the ideal, and specificity of the historical mode of existence from which the ideal world can never be completely separated, if not to be made homogeneous with the latter. Separated from the specificity of the historical, the universal claim of the ideal becomes a mere fantasm of mankind; on the other hand, the exhaustive enclosure of our existence into the particularity of the given, without any transcendence, encloses life in law. What we must be able to do, so argues Gill, is to conceive a mediated mode of existence in a dialectical manner, without any totalizing meta-narrative. The questions of reason and truth in religion and politics must be understood from this dialectically mediated thinking that brings together, without totality, the universal thrust of the ideal and singular insistence on what is irreducibly historical and embedded. The question of life is fundamental to Soumick De's paper as well. Reading St. Augustine, Soumick seeks to conceive of life that cannot be enclosed in the cages of law without remainder. It is from this perspective, Soumick attempts to formulate what he calls "philosophy of use" in conjunction with desire, a nexus at the heart of which lies love that opens, from the depth of finitude, to the infinite released from the bounds of law, an idea that he thinks to be fundamental to St. Augustine's Christian philosophy of love.

In his essay *Beyond Protective Discoloration: Ambedkar on Conversion,* Soumyabrata Choudhury reflects on the Ambedkar question of conversion "with a new tool of thought", namely, theory of names. Taking his inspiration from some of the important contemporary thinkers such as Giorgio Agamben and Alain Badiou, Choudhury argues that Ambedkar's thought on conversion opens us to the thought of a generic and universal potentiality that each time opens up a neo name which is not "an unknown new name [that] one invents, [but] the unknown *in* the known names". In that manner, the neo name escapes from the totalizing juridico-political narrative that conjures up a new name only to enclose it within the categorical imperative of the juridical. In a different registrar but in a certain affinity with Choudhury's paper, Achia Anzi's paper attempts to think the question of religion anew, in the wake of Georges Bataille's thinking. Religion here appears in its radical potentiality as potentiality, not as one theoretical or juridico-political option among others—choices that restitutes rather than radically subverts "the order of things"—but as the very existential opening up of being beyond "the order of things". Religion in a fundamental sense is to be understood, less as one sociological-cultural phenomenon among others, but as that which opens up the elemental nudity of being, as if it were a desert, where alone a plenitude and "fullness", repressed in the order of things, can at all arrive. In his graphic essay, *History and Eschatology: The Puranic Trait in Indo-Islamic Allegory,* Milind Wakankar conceives of a limit of worldly experience in a manner—contra Erich Auerbach—that is "counter-figural". Wakankar calls such "counter-figural" limit experience, which is not accessible to an empirical-historiography, as "eschatological". He thus takes Indo-Islamic allegory to test his counter-figural thinking which will reveal some surprises for the reader.

Dhananjay Singh's thoughtful paper on 3rd century Buddhist thinker Nagarjuna opens up the possibility of reading Nagarjuna as a thinker of radical difference—of what he calls "pairing"—that suspends any attempt at absolutisation of one element of "dependent origin". Thus the middle path that Nagarjuna advocates renders every approach to the unconditioned as merely provisional and precarious, bereft of ultimate normative obligations, and thus always falling short of sovereignty. Hegemonies thus lose the sense of ultimate for us. In Nagarjuna's deconstruction of immanent constitution of self, lies the immense ethico-political significance. "The full implication of Nagarjuna's assertion is", writes Dhananjay, "that he [Nagarjuna] is even rejecting any possibility of idea and ideology as it would inevitably be first based upon the absolute or permanent identity of self, thing, event or conversely upon absolute difference of one entity from the other. This particular assertion of the philosopher is extremely relevant to political discourses, which seek to gain power by employing the notions of identity and difference. Political ideologies consolidate power by propagating identity or oneness of all thereby to crush differential particularities of existence. On the other hand, they consolidate power by positing absolute non-existence of anything or everything."

The essay of Franson Manjali, titled *Nationalism, Colonialism and 'Modern Linguistics'* is an interesting genealogical investigation of the discourse called "linguistics". In this essay Manjali shows how the emergence of modern linguistics as a discourse is tied up with the rise of nationalisms in the European context and that the phenomenon of nationalisms cannot be separated from accompanied phenomenon of colonialism of the "Orient". Language is here understood neither in its instrumental-functional sense as mere transparent medium of communication and signification, nor in the scientific-objectifying sense which perceives language in its universal structure, but as a dynamic movement that inter-links various phenomena of "human" socio-political existence that can never be fixed in any logical-grammatical categories of judgment and cognition. In that sense, the phenomenon called "language" and the phenomenon called "linguistics" are profoundly historical phenomena; they can't be understood without taking into account the changing apparatuses of socio-historical epochs that determine what is meaningful and what is not.

1

Political Theology without Sovereignty: Reading Derrida Reading Religion

Clayton Crockett

In his recent book *Miracle and Machine: Jacques Derrida and the Two Sources of Religion, Science, and the Media*, Michael Naas offers a close reading of Jacques Derrida's 1996 essay "Faith and Knowledge: The Two Sources of Religion at the Limits of Reason Alone." Naas shows how these two sources of religion, the miraculous and the machinic, constitute what Derrida calls "religion" as faith and as the sacred. Furthermore, Naas traces these themes of miracle and machine across Derrida's corpus and shows how these questions related to religion animate Derrida's philosophy from the beginning to the end of his life. In addition, Naas intersperses his readings of Derrida on religion with some extraordinary connections to and reflections on Don Delillo's novel, *Underworld.*

I want to endorse Naas's reading of Derrida on religion, and his insistence on the two sources of Derrida's thinking about religion, and the role of religion in the contemporary world. In some ways Derrida is a "religious" thinker, but his religiosity is not simply equivalent to any specific religion. Naas explains that Derrida uses words like faith, God, and messianicity "in ways that court misunderstanding," but they are related to how Naas articulates the term miracle in his book. According to Naas, "Derrida says that we are called upon to believe every testimony—every claim to truth, every claim that one is telling the truth about what one knows, believes, or sees—as an 'extraordinary story' or a miracle" (Naas 2012, p. 97). The problem with the miracle, however, is that owing to repetition it is always caught up in a kind of machine. "Derrida says that the machine is simply another way of speaking about calculation and repetition, but about a calculation and repetition in relationship always to the incalculable and the unforeseeable" (Ibid., p. 118). This machinic repetition of the miracle both ruins the singularly miraculous quality of the miracle and also at the same time paradoxically makes it possible in the first place.

In amplifying Derrida's work by re-turning to and opening up this profoundly important text on religion, Naas helps us assess not only Derrida's philosophy but how it is that we can think and think about religion today. In his conclusion, Naas borrows an image in the form of a specific billboard sign from *Underworld*, and claims that in their inextricable intersection, faith and knowledge, or miracle and machine, compose a sign that reads: "Space Available." Naas reads this sign as "an affirmation that, for the moment, there is still time, and in the words of the sign itself, which can be read as the translation of either "messianicity without messianism" or *khôra*, still SPACE AVAILABLE" (Ibid., p. 275).

In my reading, I want to focus more explicitly on a theme that Naas raises over the course of a few pages, but does not fully elaborate, which is sovereignty. Derrida's religious writings are always connected to his political reflections, specifically the attempt to elaborate a "democracy to come" that would not be constituted in terms of sovereignty. According to Naas, the oneness or indivisibility of the sovereign is the legacy of a particular religion—Christianity—and a particular political history—Western European, that needs to be contested and deconstructed. As Naas says,

> Throughout the 1980s and 1990s and right up to his death, Derrida relentlessly pursued a kind of radical or originary secularism or secularity that constantly questions and criticizes the imposition of any particular religion or religious doctrine upon political concepts. Motivated in part by the analyses of Carl Schmitt, Derrida takes up

> the project of demonstrating the onto-theological origins of what at first appear to be modern secular concepts such as popular sovereignty, democracy, and religious tolerance (Ibid., p. 191).

On this reading, a Christian political theology, or the intertwining of the "theologico-political," is wrapped around sovereignty. Derrida both appreciates the incisiveness of Schmitt's analysis of political theology in *Political Theology*, and he wants to criticize and oppose Schmitt's conception of politics, most explicitly in *The Politics of Friendship*. My argument is that Derrida is working to deconstruct or dismantle the sovereignty that undergirds the political theology of Carl Schmitt. At the same time, Derrida is attentive to the inextricability of something like a theology in all politics, and the impossibility of completely separating questions of religion from questions of politics. Furthermore I suggest that this thematic of the critique or deconstruction of sovereignty animates Derrida's text on "Faith and Knowledge," even if it is less explicitly foregrounded in this essay.

In my reading I am setting up an arc for Derrida's later work that stretches from *The Politics of Friendship* and includes *Specters of Marx* (and really begins with his 1989 essay "Force of Law: The Mystical Foundation of Authority") to his later book *Rogues* and his two-volume lecture course on *The Beast and the Sovereign* around the theme of the deconstruction of sovereignty and the possibility of undoing this "theologico-political" link. I will focus briefly on Schmitt's famous text *Political Theology*, whose subtitle is "Four Chapters on the Concept of Sovereignty," and then consider some relevant passages from *The Politics of Friendship*, *The Beast and the Sovereign*, and *Rogues*. Derrida's essay "Faith and Knowledge," along with Naas's reading of it, remains in the background.

I claim that in his later work Derrida is trying to sketch out a political theology without sovereignty that would counter the political theology of Carl Schmitt, which is essentially tied to a form of sovereignty. The crucial question, for me, is whether a thinking about religion and politics that lacks any traditional notion of sovereignty would still be a political theology, or whether Schmitt's version of political theology is exhaustive.

In *Political Theology*, published in 1922, Schmitt famously claims that "all significant concepts of the modern theory of the state are secularized theological concepts," and this is not only due to their "historical development," but also has to do with their "systematic structure" (Schmitt 2005, p. 36). In this third chapter, Schmitt argues for a sociology of concepts that takes into account the genuine significance of ideas. He claims that during the modern period of European intellectual history, the battle against God represents an attack on transcendence for the sake of immanence, and this issues in modern atheism. In their attack on liberal atheism, conservative counter-revolutionary religious thinkers like Donoso Cortés reveal what is importantly at stake in this transformation. It is not simply theism vs. atheism; the problem for Schmitt is that liberal democracy represents an "onslaught against the political" (Ibid., p. 65).

The revolt against God ends up destroying not only religion but politics as well. Why? Because our understanding of God is tied to a modern conception of sovereignty and the basis of sovereignty is its decision-making capacity. The first sentence of *Political Theology* reads: "Sovereign is he who decides on the exception" (Ibid., p. 5). A decision has to be a sovereign decision to be a true political decision. Schmitt criticizes the degeneration of modern law and economics to the point where it attempts to eradicate the need for any decision. This elimination of the decision is both impossible and undesirable. At the end of the book, he argues that

> Whereas, on the one hand, the political vanishes into the economic or technical-organizational, on the other hand the political dissolves into the everlasting discussion of cultural and philosophical-historical commonplaces, which, by aesthetic characterization, identify and accept an epoch as classical, romantic, or baroque. The core of the political idea, the exacting moral decision, is evaded in both (Ibid., p. 65).

Sovereignty is tied to the possibility of a political decision. In overthrowing the sovereignty of God, humans are attempting to get rid of sovereignty altogether. But this effort eliminates all politics, which Schmitt wants to hold onto. Politics requires the sovereign decision in order to be morally exacting, and there is always a residual structure of the theological in every moral-political decision.

In his book written later in the 1920s, *The Concept of the Political*, Schmitt further clarifies what he means by the political, which is the famous distinction between friend and enemy.[1] It is the ability to make such a distinction that renders an action political or morally exacting in its highest sense. And it is the ability to make such a clear and absolute distinction that Derrida contests in *The Politics of Friendship*. Derrida suggests that an opposition between friend and enemy of the sort that Schmitt sets up necessarily deconstructs. There is an aporia in the event of a political decision that ruins sovereignty at the same time as it upholds it. For Schmitt, politics depends on the decision concerning who is a friend and who is an enemy, and the enemy is then the object of political hatred and war. Derrida notes "the fundamentally Christian politics" of Schmitt, that is only possible when thought under a "Christian metaphysics of subjectivity" (Derrida 1997, pp. 84 and 243).

According to Derrida, the sovereign decision is ruined from within by the aporia of responsibility. He argues that "*a theory of the subject*" such as Schmitt's "*is incapable of accounting for the slightest decision*" (Ibid., p. 68 (emphasis in original). This is because every active or autonomous decision is also exposed to a passive decision as its necessary condition. "The passive decision," Derrida writes, "condition of the event, is always in me, structurally, another event, a rending decision as the decision of the other" (Ibid). Schmitt's political theology cannot account for this other decision that inhabits and wrecks the sovereign decision that decides on the exception. Derrida says that "the decision is not only always exceptional, *it makes an exception of/for me*" (Ibid., p. 69). The sovereign decision makes an exception for me, and I have the power to decide, but this decision "exonerates from no responsibility." Responsibility, which lies at the heart of Derrida's faith, as one of the two sources of religion, means that I am "responsible from myself before the other, I am first of all and also responsible *for the other before the other*" (Ibid.). The temptation is to read this responsibility as a moral exhortation, but for Derrida it is a much deeper and more structural situation that he develops from the philosophy of Lévinas, and this responsibility constitutes the self as self. As the Indian philosopher Saitya Brata Das explains, Derrida "speaks of a messianic exception which for him is the true exception, and which is different from the exceptionality of the sovereign in respect to law" (Das 2013, p. 14)).

Derrida wants to avoid or overcome the Christian metaphysics and politics of Schmitt, but he understands that there is an irreducible religious element to all politics and all philosophy, so he adopts the term messianic, or "messianicity without messianism" as he articulates it in *Specters of Marx*. The human being is marked by this exceptional messianicity and this unavoidable responsibility, divided and shared as she is between a pure animal and an absolute sovereign. In his two-volume lecture course on *The Beast and the Sovereign*, Derrida tracks these themes through Western literary and philosophical discourse. In Volume I, he claims that he is working against Schmitt's "cunning intensification of the political" that relies on a conception of evil by which to judge the political enemy, but he affirms "an other politicization" rather than a de-politicization, "and therefore another concept of the political" (Derrida 2009, p. 75). This other concept of the politics is based on a deconstruction of sovereignty. For Derrida, sovereignty is not indivisible; it is divisible and divided. And "a divisible sovereignty is no longer a sovereignty, a sovereignty worthy of the name, i.e. pure and unconditional" (Ibid., pp. 76-77). It is not enough to simply change subjects or exchange sovereigns from God to monarch to people: "The sovereignty of the people or of the nation merely inaugurates a new form of the same fundamental structure" (Ibid., p. 282). So the deconstruction of sovereignty issues not in a liberal democracy, however politicized. Derrida affirms a more radical form of democracy, a democracy *to come*.

Schmitt takes aim, along with many other conservative and radical critics, at liberal democracy. He offers a scornful dismissal of liberalism in *Political Theology* to the effect that "liberalism...existed...only in that short period in which it was possible to answer the question 'Christ or Barabbas?' with a proposal to adjourn or to appoint a commission of investigation" (Schmitt 2005,

p. 62). In a similar vein, Alain Badiou rails against contemporary parliamentary democracies and their inability to recognize radical evil (Badiou 2005, p. 20). Derrida does not want to defend liberal or parliamentary democracy, but he does want to save the name of democracy, and to inflect it more futural terms.

In his book *Rogues*, Derrida shows how the question of democracy is still necessarily caught up with the question of God, even if he wants to think of both democracy and divinity without sovereignty. Most contemporary reflections on democracy see it as tied to a form of sovereignty. He says that "now, democracy would be precisely this, a force (*kratos*) a force in the form of a sovereign authority..., and thus the power and ipseity of the people (*demos*)" (Derrida 2005, p. 13). Is it possible to have democracy without sovereignty, and if so, what would that mean? The problem is that any sovereignty necessarily involves the One, the authority of the One who acts and decides, whether the sovereign is God or King or People. Even if democratic sovereignty relies on the sovereignty of the people, it retains "the sovereignty of the One...above and beyond the dispersion of the plural"(Ibid., p. 16). A state-form that relies on any form of sovereignty is in some respects a rogue state, because the force of sovereign authority ultimately comes down to the "reason of the strongest" (Ibid., p. 18). For Derrida, an affirmation of democracy would have to mean a dispersal of the One, a sending off and away of sovereignty, which means that democracy is never simply present but always also futural, "to come." This futurity at the heart of the present is also a kind of messianicity insofar as it is never fully present, but also gestured towards as in to the arrival of an apparition, or a ghost.

A post-sovereign democracy would have to be plural; it would have to pluralize and thus dislocate or deconstruct sovereignty, especially the sovereignty of the One. Schmitt's political theology affirms the sovereign act as a way to maintain the integrity and seriousness of politics. But Derrida attempts to think politics beyond or without sovereignty, without the sovereign one that possesses the authority to make a genuine political decision. This attempt destroys realist power politics, but it remains a vital hope for any person or people who strive for justice. A politics based on justice in the Derridean sense has to affirm democracy, not as an actual state of affairs, but as Derrida explains, "the democracy to come would be like the *khôra* of the political" (Ibid., p. 82). *Khôra* is the space available for political negotiation, that resists the closing in on itself of a sovereign One.

Derrida wonders whether his understanding of democracy and his advocating of a "democracy to-come" "might not lead back to or be reducible to some unavowed theologism" (Ibid., p. 110). Politics cannot be completely dissociated from religion, and there is a religious messianicity that haunts all our politics, even if we can keep politics from degenerating into this or that messianism. He asks, "the democracy to come, will this be a god to come? Or more than one? Will this be the name to come of a god or of democracy? Utopia? Prayer? Pious wish? Oath? Or something else altogether?" (Ibid., p. 77).[2] Derrida suggests that democracy has some connection to Heidegger's late thinking about God, as expressed in the posthumous interview, "Only a God Can Save Us," even though Heidegger resists such a connection. By reflecting carefully about his own complicated relationship to Heidegger, Derrida concludes his essay by suggesting that his own (Derrida's) understanding of democracy is tied to the idea "of a god without sovereignty," even though "nothing is less sure than his coming, to be sure" (Ibid., p. 114). Nothing is less sure than a god who could save us, even if that is the only thing that can save us now. And nothing is less sure than a democracy to come, even if that is the only hope for a responsible politics.

Just as Derrida wonders whether Heidegger can avoid writing a theology, we are justified in asking whether Derrida in fact has a political theology. To be sure, he does not use that name, and I think that it mainly due to his desire to distance himself from Schmitt's political theology. But the question remains: is there only one political theology, that of Schmitt, or is there more than one? This is the question, and the promise, of Jeffrey W. Robbins' book *Radical Democracy and Political Theology*, that seeks to develop a political theology which would not be Schmittean. Robbins relies on the work of Michael Hardt and Antonio Negri to articulate a political theology of the multitude that constitutes a radical form of democracy rather than a unitary sovereign power. Robbins cites Derrida's criticism of Schmitt in *The Politics of Friendship*, and claims that this encounter "leaves us with the question of whether a political theology might provide the necessary supplement to contemporary democratic theory and practice without falling prey to the same exclusive logic as Schmitt" (Robbins 2011, p. 113). I want to suggest that this is partly what Derrida is trying to do, but he avoids the phrase political theology for the same reason that so many theorists do, because of the long shadow cast on European radical thought by Carl Schmitt. According to Antonio Negri, whose philosophy Robbins draws upon heavily in his book, there is only "just one political theology, the one at whose opposite ends stand Bodin and Stalin, with Carl Schmitt occupying a slot somewhere in between" (Negri 2013, p. 32). If Negri is right, then Robbins is wrong, and there is no possibility for any political theology without sovereignty, because sovereignty *defines* political theology.[3]

Derrida opposes political theology in name, but he also recognizes how religion cannot be exorcised from politics, from "Force of Law" to his last writings. Instead of political theology, he works with the quasi-religious category of messianicity, "messianicity without messianism", because it is a "weaker," or less sovereign power. In a 1994 essay, "Taking a Stand for Algeria," Derrida takes "a stand for the effective dissociation of the political and the theological." He states that "our idea of democracy implies a separation between the state and the religious powers, that is, a radical religious neutrality and a faultless tolerance which would not only set the sense of belonging to religions, cults, and thus also cultures and languages, away from the reach of any terror...but also protects the practices of faith, and, in this instance, the freedom of discussion and interpretation within each religion" (Derrida 2002, pp. 301-308; quote p. 306). The religious power that the theological represents, when aligned with the political force of the state, produces terror.

Does political theology necessarily imply this sovereign power and therefore a rogue state with its concomitant violence and terror? Perhaps. But what if the theological itself could be weakened, or viewed as non-sovereign, as John D. Caputo has been insisting for years, following Derrida? In *The Weakness of God*, Caputo articulates a thinking of divinity without sovereignty. Here God names the unconditional solicitation of an event rather than

> a being who is there, an entity trapped in being, even a super-being up there, up above the world, who physically powers and causes it, who made it and occasionally intervenes upon its day-to-day activities to tweak things for the better in response to a steady stream of solicitations from down below (Caputo 2006, p. 39).

In his latest book, *The Insistence of God*, Caputo argues for a theology of "perhaps," that is tied to a weak non-sovereign force rather than traditional sovereign power. As he explains, "the 'perhaps' of which I speak here does not belong to the 'strong' or sovereign order of presence, power, principle, essence, actuality, knowledge, or belief" (Caputo 2013, p. 4). *Perhaps* means a way to say yes to the future while affirming the "chance of the event," the chance that the event might not happen as well as the chance that the event might not be what we want, or even good; it might be the worst.

According to Derrida, sovereignty is a circular movement; he says that it forms a kind of merry-go-round, a rotary motion that draws power in towards itself and then distributes this same power that it has appropriated for itself back out to the rest of us who are non-sovereign. Now, today, much of this sovereignty has become invisible; we exist in what Deleuze calls a society of control where most of the time we consist of relay points for the distribution and redistribution of sovereignty. The focal point or centre of sovereignty is invisible, it appears not to exist, but it functions all-the-more smoothly despite this inexistence. The centre of sovereignty is everywhere and nowhere, and its operation seems ubiquitous and invisible, like the spirit of God. How do we track down the machinations of sovereignty so that we can understand and perhaps even disable it, render it inoperable?

Is what Derrida calls the unconditional or the messianic a new form of sovereignty, precisely because it is undeconstructable? It is a pure force and it keeps us awaiting, expecting the unexpected and the unbelievable, like the end of the nation-state or the collapse of global capitalism. Is our faith in God or in democracy precisely what keeps us from resisting or is it what gives us the power to fight back, or is it instead what gives us the strength to resist actually the onslaught of actually existing corporate capitalism? These questions are literally undecidable but nevertheless imperative to think and to think through.

Who makes an authentic decision today? God, the autonomous self, the anonymous media, the nation, the market, or the brain? And what criteria can be applied to determine whether this decision is for the best, or at least for the better? Derrida's faith is that there are not only multiple decisions but always more than just one decider, and that this irreducible plurality at the heart of decision prevents the worst concentration of power in the hands of the One. It is the only hope for democracy, if there is such a thing.

NOTES

1. "The specific political distinction to which political actions and motives can be reduced is that between friend and enemy" (Schmitt 1996, p. 26).
2. See my suggestion that this god could be viewed less in terms of Judeo-Christian divinity than as an African or Caribbean orisa or lwa (Crockett 2013, pp. 185-194).
3. Paul Kahn updates Schmitt and applies his work to the United States. Kahn's understanding of political theology is based ultimately on the idea of sacrifice, but here sacrifice reinforces rather than dismantles sovereignty (Kahn 2011).

REFERENCES

Badiou, Alain, *Metapolitics*, trans. Jason Barker (New York: Verso, 2005).

Caputo, John D., *The Weakness of God: A Theology of the Event* (Bloomington: Indiana University Press, 2006).

Caputo, John D., *The Insistence of God: A Theology of Perhaps* (Bloomington: Indiana University Press, 2013).

Crockett, Clayton, "Vodou Economics: Haiti and the Future of Democracy," in *Deleuze Beyond Badiou: Ontology, Multiplicity and Event* (New York: Columbia University Press, 2013), pp. 185-194.

Das, Saitya Brata, *The Wounded World: Essays on Ethics and Politics* (Delhi: Aakar Books, 2013).

Derrida, Jacques, *The Politics of Friendship*, trans. George Collins (London: Verso, 1997)

Derrida, Jacques, "Taking a Stand for Algeria," trans. Boris Belay, in *Acts of Religion*, ed. Gil Anidjar (London: Routledge, 2002).

Derrida, Jacques, *The Beast and the Sovereign,* Volume I, trans. Geoffrey Bennington (Chicago: University of Chicago Press, 2009).

Derrida, Jacques, *Rogues: Two Essays on Reason*, trans. Pascale-Anne Brault and Michael Naas (Stanford: Stanford University Press, 2005).

Kahn, Paul, *Political Theology: Four New Chapters on the Concept of Sovereignty* (New York: Columbia University Press, 2011).

Naas, Michael, *Miracle and Machine: Jacques Derrida and the Two Sources of Religion, Science and the Media* (Fordham University Press, 2012).

Negri, Antonio, *Spinoza for Our Time: Politics and Postmodernity*, trans. William McCuaig (New York: Columbia University Press, 2013).

Robbins, Jeffrey W., *Radical Democracy and Political Theology* (New York: Columbia University Press, 2011).

Schmitt, Carl, *Political Theology: Four Chapters on the Concept of Sovereignty*, trans. George Schwab (Chicago: University of Chicago Press, 2005).

Schmitt, Carl, *The Concept of the Political*, trans. George Schwab (Chicago: University of Chicago Press, 1996).

2

Truth and Reason in Religion and Politics

Harjeet Singh Gill

In philosophical understanding Truth and Reason are ideas which are applicable to all institutions of religion and politics. From the very beginning this philosophical enquiry begins with our comprehension of specific situations based on sensuous experiences. The Socratic dialogues attempt to explore all empirical experiences of justice, beauty, truth and ultimately come to the conclusion that only the Ideas of justice, beauty and truth are valid criteria to make any plausible judgement. The artisan makes a bed on the basis of the Idea of the bed, says Socrates. The idea of circle enables us to judge whether a given drawn circle is circular enough. The idea of beauty enables the judges to declare several objects beautiful, in spite of the fact that all these beautiful objects are physically different from each other. And, when we come to the ideal, perfect State, none of the prolonged debates lead us anywhere. Finally, it is the idea of the perfect, harmonious State that is the object of philosophical reflection. It is the soul, the intellect, the pure reason that alone can comprehend and envisage even the possibility of a State where there would be perfect harmony, where there would be no conflict of interest with an absolutely ideal and abstract communism of wives, children and property. In other words, after long and prolonged discussions, Plato ends up proposing a metaphysical State, a surrealistic State that can never be but that would be the measure of all States which aspire to be good States.

It is not surprising that several centuries later, Karl Marx begins by criticizing Hegel for his idealism with his famous Material conception of history and ends up proposing an ideal State where there would be no classes, no exploiters, no exploited, no power relations, where the State itself will wither away. This Marxist State is no less metaphysical than that of Plato.

There is another very important point to be noted here. It is the atheistic or almost atheistic undercurrent of all philosophical speculation. The pre-Socratic philosophers killed the gods when they explained all physical phenomena like thunder or rain in terms of pure physical causes and effects, not due to the fury of gods. For Socrates and Plato, there is God but this God is nothing more than a general principle of cosmic harmony. There is no personal being, the Lord, the Creator sitting somewhere in heaven that one can pray to. It is simply a metaphysical or cosmic principle, an axiom, to explain things which for the time being remain unexplainable. Strangely enough, we see this understanding even in the most religious philosophers. Take the case of Augustine, the most religious of the Western philosophers. He posits Faith as a point of departure but he insists that this faith must be followed and reinforced by reason and logic. He even goes to the extent by declaring that faith is inferior to reason. In the discussion that follows reason and truth turn out to be purely metaphysical concepts. Later on, Spinoza makes a clear distinction between facts and concepts.

Like Karl Marx, Kierkegaard criticized Hegel for his idealistic conception of history. He argued against Hegel that human existence cannot be comprehended in terms of Hegelian logic of the universal Idea but when he meditated on the nature of existence, he was no less metaphysical. His notions of anguish and alienation are not so different from those of Hegel or Augustine or Plato. In each case, there are mental and not physical states of consciousness. Kierkegaardian existence is not just a physical phenomenon, not even of Sartre, for that matter, it is a highly internalized metaphysical realization of alienation or *nausée*. It must be emphasized that not everybody is afflicted with this consciousness. It is a highly spiritual, cosmological experience whether the individual in question is a believer or an atheist. The different philosophical traditions in phenomenology also focus on the concept of transcendence. Every fact or phenomenon is transcended, and it is in its transcendence its signification is realized.

After this introductory note we come to specific religions and states. Every religion is a specific religion with its specific rites and rituals, rules and regulations, sacred and profane domains. There is specificity but there are also, at least in principle, some concepts, some ideas which are supposed to be universal. This is the basic predicament in all religions and cultural traditions. If there is a conflict between Augustine, the Christian, and Augustine, the neo-Platonic philosopher, it applies to all traditions. After all, even Plato's Idea also emerges from the Greek tradition. The universality is there but it is not devoid of Greek specificity. Whatever universal claim Hindu philosophy may have, it is certainly entrenched in Hindu cosmology. On the one hand, to be a Hindu or a Muslim or a Christian, and also to be a philosopher, is a major conceptual contradiction. On the other, all thinking, all philosophizing is contextual. The philosophers try to transcend this context but a close examination will show that whether it is the phenomenology of Husserl and Heidegger or existentialism of Kierkegaard or Sartre, it is squarely situated within their specific philosophical traditions. The universality as such is a misnomer. Even the most independent and original philosophers are condemned to their specific material and conceptual traditions. Karl Marx could go beyond the ideal contradictions of Hegel but he was stuck with the so-called inherent contradictions in an industrialized society, the rest was the Asiatic mode of production. It was up to Mao Zedong, a product of agrarian society, to show a hierarchy of contradictions in the Chinese social and economic structure which was considered a great theoretical development in the history of the principle of contradictions by Louis Althusser.

The so-called universal ideas have their specificity. The idea of a bed that Plato refers to, that is, the basis of the Greek artisan is not the same in India or China or Africa, if we reconstruct the history of the designs of a bed or a chair in these respective cultures. There is always a dialectical relation between the empirical forms and the abstract, conceptual forms. Nothing is created in a void. The incessant dialectical interaction between the real and the imagined, between the factual and the conceptual is the basis of all historical development in the ideas of justice and truth. There is a direct correspondence between theory and praxis. Even the most primitive ritual is explained in terms of a certain cosmology. Even the most rudimentary social organization is supported by a cosmic authority. The manifest is controlled by the immanent but its reciprocal praxis is also equally true.

In spite of all the idealism of Plato or Hegel or Marx, there is no such thing as an ideal State. It is always a Greek, a Jewish, a Christian, a Hindu, a Muslim State. The so-called universal idea of a State is a resultant of dialectic of the real and the imagined within the philosophical confines of anthropology. One should never underestimate the most powerful confines of tradition which unfortunately are both visible and invisible, both manifest and immanent. Even the rebels rebel within and against their own tradition. This is why a Christian atheist, a Hindu atheist, a Muslim atheist represent different forms of atheism. The aesthetics, the ethics, the cosmological and anthropological forms have different manifest and immanent contours in each case. Even the most manifest form of a culture, its language, is not just a grammatical construct; it has its corresponding conceptual construct with its very specific semiotic universe. We can always transcend these formal contours but this transcendence, like the philosophical transcendence of an atheist or of a phenomenologist, somehow remains within the same horizon, however abstract that horizon may be.

3

History and Eschatology: The Puranic Trait in Indo-Islamic Allegory

Milind Wakankar

I want to suggest in this paper that the eschatological limit of worldly experience can be counter-figural; instead of alluding to a point of transformation in the future, it may well refer back to a point in the past.[1] It seems to me that this point, when positioned in a past prior to thc historiographically accessible past, is pre-eminently an internal limit. An alternative history of the subject is possible here, one that is nothing if not theologico-political in its underpinnings.

To detect the traces of this millennial transformation, I begin with the saintly life of the child-devotee Prahlada. Our excursus on the life of Prahlada will take us into the heart of a typically 'Puranic' text. The Puranas, written in Sanskrit verse, were composed in the latter half of the first millennium of our common era. The date is enough to make us realize that what we have before us are not merely vast narrative sagas inflected here by doctrine and there by narrative. For there is nothing indifferent in the Puranas: they attend at every step to the problem of the relation between the internal limit to human life which is the speculative spirit and the external limit which is the world of nature experienced in space and time. Coming as they do at the end of a long millennium of philosophical speculation on this question, they quite understandably devote themselves to a narrative resolution of this problem. But what does narrative imply in this context? We will have to understand narrative as more than doctrine but also more than myth. So that what is needed here is neither a mere listing of the philosophical schools the Puranas make reference to; nor is this a matter of myth analysis. I will argue that the narratival project of the Puranas is the work of *muthos* in the expansive sense of that Greek word: it is the recapitulation of a past prior to the past available to history. More to the point, it is the recovery of the "fact" of that past. Not surprisingly the miracle of such a past translates into what is in the Puranas, a remarkable set of theses on the problem of divinity. But as we know from the Purana-scholar whose book-length essay on Prahlada I will have occasional recourse to here—I am thinking of Paul Hacker, who wrote the essay in the late 1950s (Hacker 1959)—the Puranas practise a peculiar form of ambivalence wherein, at every stage, one finds them unable to decide between the eternality of the inner world of the spirit and the transient but knowable outer world. The idea of divinity in the Puranas is by this token couched in the narratival account of this ambivalence, often with deeply unsettling effects, as we will see in the case of Prahlada.

Hacker's magisterial essay traces the Prahlada story in its many recensions from the Mahabharata down to the Bhagavata Purana, which is the locus classicus of what is known as Vaisnava or Bhagavata dharma, the tradition of Visnu-worship. Let us stay with the story as it appears in its most developed form in Canto Seven of the latter text, which was composed by Tamil Alwar poets at some point in the 8th century (1993); I will not make reference to Prahlada as he appears in a text that is exactly antecedent to the Bhagavat, which is the Visnu Purana (CE 1-4th century). The myth itself is easily recounted. Enraged by Visnu's killing (in his boar-avatar) of his brother Hiranyaksha, the demon-king Hiranyakashipu undertakes an unprecedented form of penance. Disconcerted by the sheer force of his ascetic passion, the gods appeal to Brahma to grant him a boon. Here is what the demon-king asks for: "Give me the power to be lord over all creatures. Grant that no created being, whether man or animal, organic or inorganic, god or demon can bring about my death. Grant that my death take place beyond the antinomies of outside and inside, day and night, caused by beings neither terrestrial nor otherwise, and neither on earth nor in heaven." The boon is granted. Then begins a long period of tyranny characterized by Hiranyakashipu's persecution of Brahmanical society, mostly by the devastation of its ritual every day. This is followed by the persecution of his own son Prahlada when, in catechism after catechism, the latter betrays a profound knowledge and fealty to Visnu. He cannot but deny the sovereignty of Hiranyakashipu, for he knows only one lord, Visnu himself. His demon-father is enraged and subjects Prahlada to a series of trials of a brutal variety, going so far as to throw him into a pit of snakes. The child survives every test by dint of his devotion to Visnu. As a final affirmation of his love for his devotee Visnu himself appears in an extraordinary deus ex machina. In this well known Puranic scene, the god defies the limitations imposed by Brahma's boon, but in a highly unusual way. He emerges from within a pillar at twilight, though not as Visnu but as a creature half man and half lion. In this anthropo-feline (*Narsimha*) avatar, having incised the antinomic cordon around Hiranyakashipu, the god holds the demon-king on his knee and proceeds to disembowel him. Prahlada is anointed the new demon-king.

It should be clear from this sketch that the tale is steeped in a kind of passionate intensity that can only produce an unprecedented dramatic conflict. There is the deep melancholy of Hiranyakashipu and his family upon the death of his brother. This is followed by the ardour of his penance, instituted to avenge himself on Visnu and to challenge the latter's sovereign sway over the three worlds. Counterposed to this range of passions is the fervour of Prahlada, whose sermons on the nature and essence of Visnu as godhead acquire an almost apocalyptic tenor under the force of his father's intransigence. All these signs indicate that the text is not merely a Vaisnava hagiography. In point of fact, it puts into play a central paradox that calls to be incised and reconciled by the pacific figure of Prahlada.

The paradox is introduced by the text in the frame narrative that has King Parikshit in conversation with Suka. This is how the issue is broached at the very beginning of the Canto Seven (I present the two verses in prose):

> Parikshit: God (*bhagwan*) loves all beings (*priyaha...bhutanam*), is in empathy (*suhrida*) with them, wants to be non-indifferent (*sama*) with them. Why then would he take sides, pitting himself against foes for the sake of Indra, going so far as to enter into indifference (*visama*) with them? If God's essence is to be the unmediate salve (*saksan nihisreyasa*), he can have no sociality of interest (*hasyartha*) with gods. [Conversely,] as a being without qualities (*agunasya*), [which is to say, none derived from primordial matter,] he cannot harbour any impetuosity (*udvega*) or enmity (*vidvesa*) towards demons. [BP 7:1:1-2.]

For Parikshit as for Prahlada, Visnu is undoubtedly one with all beings, but this oneness is not indifferent in quality. He is not merely the common element in a manifold of beings. Visnu is qualitatively different, he is the highest of the high. For this reason, Visnu is nothing if not this movement between the one *in* the many and the one *as against* the many. Gods and demons inhabit the realm of the indifferent (*visama*)—gods as beings requiring other grounds for their authority, demons as the very instance of beings determined by different *gunas* (qualities, moods)—but Visnu's soteriology needs no mediation just as his being can have no connection with the sensible world of the three *gunas* (*sattva*, *rajas* and *tamas*).

Now the question is: what explains God's need to descend into the polemical standoff between a friend and an enemy? By way of a response, Suka cites Narada, the messenger of the gods, who had replied to a similar query from King Yudhistir. (In the embedded narrative that follows from this point in Canto Seven, it is Narada who then proceeds to recite the saintly tale of Prahlada for Yudhistir's edification.)

> Narada: Yudhistir! It is my firm view that the extent to which man can unite (*tanmayata*) with God in a stance of enmity (*vairanubandhena*) is unmatched even by the yoking [with God] effected by [the participant devotion which is] bhakti. A wasp having

> entrapped a worm on a wall, the worm in fevered anxiety contemplates (*tamanusmaran*) the wasp with fear—thus does the worm by turns acquire the same form (*tatsarupatama*) as the wasp. [BP 7: 1: 26-27.]

By token of this contemplation (*smarana*, *tanmayata*), what is indifferent (*visama*) to God becomes non-indifferent (*sama*, *tatsarupatama*). Enemies of Visnu may well be reborn as his enemies in his successive avataras, but they will all by sheer force of this inimical obsession have finally merged with him (BP 7:1; 32-46). Following Schelling's use of the word in his *Ages of the World* drafts, we can think of this thinking-after as a kind of obsession, a *Sehnsucht* (Schelling 2000/1815). (I will explain shortly why the parallel with Schelling is both appropriate and useful.) It is almost as though the world of the enemies of Visnu, one that is at once inimical and polemical, asks at the very limit of its hateful passion to unite in infatuation with its object.

An obsessive hatefulness towards God is then not very different, is perhaps more effective, than an obsessively devotional comportment towards him. This is the gist of a framing device couching a tale that, at least on the face of it, is almost entirely about the obsessive devotion (*smarana*, *tanmayata*) of Prahlada! At this point it would be somewhat simplistic of us to imagine that the widening inclusiveness between frame and tale, enemy and friend is merely an aspect of Vaisnava theology. What is more crucial here is what can be called the "ontological" relation between men and gods. That relation is defined of course by the question of mortality. I mention "gods" here; but the demonology of the text moves freely between gods and demons as two forms of being that surpass humanity and its limits. To be sure, the specific demonological stake here is to enter into the problem of the relation between the internal and external world. Unfortunately for us, the inculcation of Prahlada into the pantheon as a would-be martyr-devotee for Visnu has meant that the tradition tends to neglect the exact rationale for Hiranyakashipu's hubris. This may give one the mistaken impression that the latter's overleaping of demonic power by way of Brahma's boon finds its reversal, and therefore its neutral or resolved form, in Prahlad's interiorization of Visnu through his powers of reflective recall (*smarana*). It would seem as though the text is solely about the institution of God in Prahlada's inner world, a process that at its very limits draws an analogy between Brahman (the world as interiorized essence) and Visnu as sovereign deity over the external world. But if the setting up of this thesis as an axiom ("Visnu *is* Brahman") were the sole aim of the Canto Seven we would lose sight of the philosophical *and* (I would argue) the historical problem the text sets into play.

That problem is best characterized as the obsessiveness of reason precisely in the way Schelling sought to explain it. It helps turn our sights away from Visnu as end to Visnu as the origin. Whether this origin is cosmological or cosmogonic in its implications is perhaps less important than the fact that the origin is that to which the whole trajectory of Vaisnava rationality returns. At the origin and at the end is Hiranyakashipu, not Prahlada. What is the significance of this circular return? It represents, to my mind, a specifically Puranic response to questions the tradition as a whole had had to deal with in the momentous interface between early Upanisadic thinking and the first sermons of the Buddha in late antiquity. The results of that interface were twofold. (I rely here on the influential recent account of these issues by Toshifumi Goto; see Goto 2005, pp. 71-85). One, the *Brihadaranyaka Upanisad*, as the earliest of the Upanisads, established the problem of mortality as one that was first and foremost about the end of life, or the ends of human life in general. The notion of the afterlife (a temporary stay in heaven) for the *atman* became less crucial than the problem of the return to *samsara*. Here the *atman* becomes the internal limit of reflection on the problem how to escape the cycle of rebirth; this *atman* is not the soul, nor is it the spirit; it is the point of reflexivity at which thought turns upon itself. And for this reason, *samsara* is not the world given historically (as a Christian scene of strife or redemption) but the world *as* the necessary and uncircumventible fall into rebirth. So the end of human life became co-terminus with the point of internal reflexivity (the point of institution of the *atman*). Another way of saying this is that the internal limit which was the *atman* was set in place at the point at which the external world was delimited, which is to say the natural or sensory world as the stage for the cycle of rebirth. This was the fertile ground for the theses on the *atman* put forth by the schools of Vedanta in the first millennium CE; they took as their point of departure some of the key theses (the *mahavakyas*) of the early Upanisads.

Secondly, if the emphasis in these early texts is on the reversal at the end (death as the "end" that can also be a vestibule into a life free from death), the major shift that occurred with the Buddha was a renewed meditation not on the end that is death, but on the beginning that is birth. It was no longer the question of a life free from death (*amartya*) but of a life free from (re)birth (*jati*). If the *atman* marked the internal limit of bodily existence, a remnant of the eternal in the midst of all that is transient in the world, the notion of *jati* introduced a kind of fold in the internal limit. The *atman* as the negation of death had to give way to *jati* as the negation of birth. It was only a short but momentous step from this to the idea that all origin is derived from other origins, leading to the idea of the transience of origin itself. This form of *pratityasamutpada* (dependent origination), which was the finding of the major Buddhist philosopher Nagarjuna, implied that all being passes over into nothing. Which is to say that we can free ourselves from the weight of all entanglements with the lived world if we train ourselves to focus on becoming itself. For what is retained in the eternal movement between being and nothing on the one hand, and nothing and being on the other, is minimally the transience of transience itself: this is the minimal element of life as it is lived in the awareness of perpetual movement, change and becoming.

Despite their seeming heterogeneity of content, the Puranas can be understood, as I have suggested above, to be a series of responses to these crucial ideas put in place and disseminated in late antiquity. What is the crisis that the Puranas respond to? One might characterize this is as an emerging uncertainty with regard to the status of the lived world. Let us not understand this to be a "traditional" response seeking to restore the certitudes of the Vedic period, such as were overturned by the Upanisads. The vast and complex machine of the Puranas, with all its deliberate archaisms, its many digressions, its attention to doctrine and so on, seeks instead to return to the radical notion of worldly life that is at the heart of Vedic thinking, and of the Rig Veda in particular. What this notion specifies is not the necessary movement of life into death, being into nothing and vice versa. It understands the negativity inherent in this transience, but it seeks to attend instead to the movement by which negativity itself is annulled, giving rise to some form of affirmation. We can see how there is an infinitesimal proximity here between the Puranas and the late Buddhist theses (as Hacker too has noticed). But if there is this family resemblance, there is a also a crucial difference between the Puranic and Buddhist account of negativity. If we think of the process by which being passes over into nothing as "nihilation", we can define the movement between the two as abyssal or "an-nihilative" of worldly life. This annihilative understanding of the world was the central contribution of Buddhist thinking since Nagarjuna, spawning a great number of variants in the Buddhist universe. But to highlight the minimal departure that the Puranas seek to undertake, we will have to think of "nihilation" somewhat differently.

At this point, we can return instructively to our own text. I remarked earlier that the trajectory of Vaisnava rationality in the text seeks to return not to the loving infatuation of Prahlada but to the obsessional animus of Hiranyakashipu. This is the upshot of the myth itself, especially in its final moment when Visnu as man-lion disembowels the prostrate Hiranyakshipu. Moving between friend and enemy, love and hate, Canto Seven of the Bhagavata Purana attempts to expand the idea of the non-indifference (*sama*) of Visnu outwards to the lived world of the indifferent and transient beings that can only have a negative relation to each other (*visama*). But the question is: how does one explain the fact that Visnu as man-lion is in the text posited as a reality exactly half way between Hiranyakashipu and Prahlada? Let us look at the man-lion's anomalous status as a creature that, although half-human, nonetheless bears a reference to animal life. This is to say that, the man-lion is a figure for what we can call in line with recent debates, the problem of animality. Now, the status of the animal is paradoxical. We cannot say, as does Heidegger, that a stone entirely lacks the notion of "being in the world" vouchsafed to human beings alone, but that the animal is "poor in world".[2] For to say that is at once to throw open animality to something worldly or human *and* to close that momentary aperture in the very same instance. In the same way, one could ask: why does Canto Seven present Visnu as a creature fundamentally non-indifferent (*sama*) but also and at the same time the very embodiment of the indifferent (*visama*)? It is not a matter of merely breaking through the antinomies soldered together by Brahma's boon. More is at stake, since Vaisnava thinking here wants to argue in the final instance for the non-indifference (*sama*) of friend and enemy here. Moreover, we are given to believe that at the moment when Visnu as man-lion drinks the blood of the demon-king, the latter *could not have been more proximal* than at any other time to Visnu himself. So whereas a cursory understanding of the myth would have us believe that it is Prahlada's ascendancy that is moot here, a closer look reminds us of the centrality of Hiranyakashipu to the philosophical (call it doctrinal) question at issue. The very passion of the monstrous man-lion is but a reflection of the monstrous antipathy of the demon-king. My point is that, rather than simply portray the effort of Visnu to rescue his child-devotee, Canto Seven takes pains to break through the representational possibilities made available by Puranic myth. This is then a reflexive moment, one in which hate and love, friend and enemy are reflected in each other with their differences cancelled out by virtue of the unlikely union —or strictly speaking the being-with (*sayujya*)— of the demon-king with God. One could argue that a complete overthrow of representational constraints is necessary for this famous and much re-enacted scene to occur. Hiranyakashipu's hubris, which impels him to a lordship over the spatially available universe, finds its nemesis in a complete absorption in Visnu, an absorption that is at once anomalous and regulative within the Vaisnava frame. Regulative, because Visnu must break through all the constraints imposed by Brahma's boon, constraints that have to do with the world of space and time. And anomalous, because only through his own gory disembowelment can Hiranyakashipu find a place in that inner domain where, in this Purana's Vedantic schema, Visnu and Brahman are one.

With this finding, it is time we returned to the question of nihilation. I have been arguing that the Puranas are a response to the "annihilative" dimension of Buddhist thought. I defined the latter in such terms as an insistence on the movement between being and nothing; annihilation involves an emphasis on the negativity inherent in this moment. From this perspective it is now possible for us to detect in the Puranic text a minimally different emphasis. For in the trajectory of Canto Seven, as I have tried to show, there is a deeply disturbing embrace of animus. Note that this is an embrace: animus is retained in it, not effaced in favour of divine love. I believe the key to the Puranic notion of the world lies in the fact of this retention. The implication is that the world that *is* Visnu emerges from out of the fundamental retention of the negative moment. Love and hate are not indifferently reconciled in him; we neglect the essence of divinity if we merely think of it as reconciliatory in its effects. This is in all probability an instance of our retroactive attempt to inject a humanized account of the world back into this text. For, the divine here oversees the emergence of worldliness from out of a prior negativity. Hence the central role accorded in this tale to the demonic. Its demonology, couched in the tale's dark core (which is the death of the demon-king), is the secret source of the luminous world that is finally affirmed at its culmination. Where the profound insight of Buddhist thought was to enter into the possibilities opened up by the question of annihilation, the Puranic text seems to want to bring about a new relation to nihilation itself. The notion of the world that it unveils is assuredly "inhuman", if one can use the word. The dark origin of this world is nihilation, which is to say (in the case of our myth) the unabsorbable negativity of Hiranyakashipu. The restoration of dharmic order that ensues cannot then but be a form of "un-nihilation" (I borrow the phrase from Eugen Fink).

We must remember however that this coming-from-out-of-the

dark into the light is impelled by the obsessive force of Hiranyakashipu's demonic hatred of Visnu. This fatal obsession is counterpointed in the text by the enlightened ardour of Prahlada. The demon-king's is a passion from within the dark; it is the necessary condition for the tale of the child-devotee. It is almost as though a passion of the exterior world is made to serve as the very basis, the very ground for a passion of the interior world. In other words, a benighted passion from out of the Puranic past serves as the threshold for the very instance of Vaisnava rationality that is Prahlada's brilliant series of sermons on the onto-theology of Visnu; this is the prelude to the Puranic future. Schelling's notion of obsession as *Sehnsucht* is then an apt description of this emergence. Rather than assume that the earlier moment of darkness is eclipsed by the later moment of light, Schelling tells us the earlier moment seeks to be drawn into the later. But the force of this pull is unique to that earlier moment itself: it is by an act of "love" (obsessive hate which is always already obsessive love) that it pushes itself into the open to embrace the light. More strictly, Schelling is speaking here of the relation between what he calls the prior "potency" (*Potenz*) of the natural world and the ultimate potency of the world of the spirit. To put it differently, nature contains within itself both the ground for the mystery of its own sentience as well as the ground for the future emergence of the human mind or spirit; it is not supplanted by a (human) spirit gifted with the power to contemplate the assimilation of all things within the absolute. Instead, the natural world remains the necessary (and darkly obsessional) prelude to the historical advent of the spirit. (In this schema the virulence of the man-lion serves, one might argue, as an *interlude* between nature and spirit.) Obsession then is both intensely self-directed *and* passionately other-directed towards the object opposing it.

The fact is that Visnu as the seat of an interiorized reason is not averse to the inauguration of exteriority. One must understand the latter as first and foremost a question of limits. The qualitative infinite that is Prahlada's inner devotion finds its counterpoint in the quantitative infinite that is Hiranyakashipu's unbridled rage. Linking the two is of course Visnu himself, who is the paradigm for measure (*maryada*). The man-lion represents that which is immeasurable about measure, the point where measure is equal to the absolute. But what is measure itself (measure *as* Visnu) than the threshold for the emergence of the subject? This is because of the retentive nature of Vaisnava reason, itself the source of the movement from dark to light, and from hidden to open. And so the subject of the Puranas appears as the 'I' that sought to keep to itself but was instead 'pulled' towards the world. The Puranic text would seem to be a meditation on the nature of this compulsion. The compulsion has neither origin nor end but it nonetheless generates the world from out of the void of a self-related obsession. Is that process of generation tantamount to something affirmative? The Puranas do not reply to this question: suffice to say that the entire elaborate machine of the Puranas is an answer of sorts. What it offers is not a history of the world *per se* but a history of "un-nihilation" as the scene for the emergence of the historical world.

NOTES

1. The idea of a figuration pointed to the future is the theme of Erich Auerbach's celebrated essay from 1944 "Figura", (1984, pp. 11-76) . Much of what I try to do in this paper is part of my ongoing project at writing an "Anti-Auerbach".
2. I am summarizing here Derrida's intricate reading of a passage in Heidegger's *Fundamental Concepts of Metaphysics*, a key lecture course from the period soon after *Being and Time* [1927]); see Derrida (1989, pp. 47-51).

REFERENCES

Atha Srimadbhagavatam (Varanasi: Chaukhamba Vidyabhavan, 1993).

Auerbach, Erich. "Figura" in *Scenes from the Drama of European Literature* (Minneapolis: University of Minnesota Press, 1984), pp. 11-76.

Derrida, Jacques, *Of Spirit: Heidegger and the Question*, trans. Geoffrey Bennington and Rachel Bowlby (Chicago: The University of Chicago Press, 1989).

Goto, "Yajnavalkya's Characterization of the Atman and the Four Kinds of Suffering in early Buddhism", *Electronic Journal of Vedic Studies* (*EJVS*) 12-2 (2005) 71-85.

Hacker, Paul, *Prahlada—Werden und Wandlungen einer Idealgestalt* (Wiesbaden: Franz Steiner, 1959).

Schelling, F.W.J.von, *The Ages of the World (1815)*, trans. Jason M. Wirth (Albany: State University of New York Press, 2000).

4

Schelling: Religion and Politics

Saitya Brata Das

Increasingly from his 1804 essay called *Philosophy and Religion* onwards, F.W.J. von Schelling is preoccupied with the possibility of what he calls "philosophical religion", a religion to come, and with the question concerning the future *of* religion as such. The eschatology of Schelling that found such intensity of expression in his incomplete magnum opus *The Ages of the World*, and later in his 1841/42 lectures on *Philosophy of Revelation*, understood religion itself as essentially futural. Irreducible to any and all possible enclosures of religion in the immanence of self-presence, Schelling sought to think religion in a new sense: religion as unenclosed opening to the unconditional, a sense and a passion that religion shares with philosophy. Existing in the neighbourhood to each other, philosophy and religion—each in its own manner—infinitely open us to the generosity of the unconditional which can neither be demonstrated in the predicative structure of the speculative proposition nor can it be understood on the basis of the tasks of world-historical politics. Religion and philosophy, in two fold manners, open us thereby to an unsaturated excess outside the *nomos* of the worldly powers in the profane order and outside the predicative structure of the dominant Occidental metaphysics. Reading the early philosophical works of Schelling, especially his 1804 essay *Philosophy and Religion* and 1810 Private lecture in Stuttgart, this paper argues that it is in these two works, along with his 1809 *Essay Concerning the Essence of Human Freedom*, that we find the early formulation of Schelling's eschatology.

In these essays we find Schelling understanding eschatology as infinite disclosures of the divine that constantly opens us to a future *to come* by refusing to be embodied in the immanence of the world-historical potencies. These world-historical powers thereby lose their autochthony and autarchy, their legitimacy and sovereignty to elicit from us absolute obligation. They can at best be understood as merely the orders of "passing away", as impoverished attempts of mankind to supplement of a fundamental fall (*Abfall*) that marks it essentially as historical condition. Such *fall* with which the history for mankind itself is inaugurated, will henceforth mark the world-historical powers with an indelible caesura that can never be redeemed by these world-sovereign powers themselves. This caesura will forever haunt any attempts at the strict analogy between the political and theological, the divine and the profane. For Schelling, religion is nothing other than this constant exposure of us to this abyss without which neither promise nor hope ever exist for us. Schelling thereby prepares for us a political theology without sovereignty, where religion in its spirit and promise—uncoupled from the world-historical foundation—keeps alive to an absolute beatitude *to come*, an unconditional beatitude which alone redeems mankind from the violence of history.

1. The Gift of Beatitude

Schelling's 1802-3 series of lectures on *The Philosophy of Art* begins with formulation of the task of philosophy of art that presents laws of their phenomenal apparitions as ideas. This task of the philosophy of art is distinguished from the empirical-historical construction of arts that is content in classifying the works of art under general concepts. The presentation of these ideas in a constellation is the task of intellectual intuition of the philosopher rather than objects of empirical intuition of the theoretician of art. Ideas are as irreducible to conceptual logic of subsumption as the presentation of the absolute in intellectual intuition to the theoretical representation of the particulars. Ideas as truth, in their highest mode of being, are at one with absolute beauty. What absolute beauty is, is none other than "the truth of ideas": it radiates like rays emanating from a constellation. Writes Schelling,

> Philosophy, which concerns itself only with ideas, must present only the general laws of phenomenal appearance as regards the empirical side of art, and must present these only in the form of ideas, for forms of art are the essential forms of things as they are in the archetypes. Hence, to the extent that these can be comprehended universally and from the perspective of the universe in and for itself, their presentation is a necessary part of the philosophy of art...philosophy of art in the larger sense is the presentation of the absolute world in the form of art. Only theory concerns itself directly with the particular or with goal, and only according to theory can a project be executed empirically...that which the philosophy must recognize and present in it is of a higher sort, and is one and the same with absolute beauty: the truth of ideas (Schelling 1989, p. 7).

The metaphor of constellation is indispensable to understand the early Schelling. Taking this metaphor from the Platonic theory of physics as Plato propounds in *Timaeus*, Schelling transforms the theory of ideas as essential forms of things into the theory of potencies in his philosophy of art. Absolute beauty is "the truth of ideas" which must be displayed in a constellation[1]. This vocation of the Schellingian philosopher is distinguished from the goal of a theoretician. In the presentation of ideas and in the display of their absolute beauty the works of art appear as universality without losing their singularity. This philosophical task is wholly different from a theoretician who subsumes singularity into particularity and then places them under the generality of the concept, repressing thereby the element of singularity. Intellectual intuition is here not the dark night where "all cows are black"[2], but a non-composite and non-descript disclosure of phenomena in their irreducible singularity holding together universality. It is nondescript because this simultaneity at the same constitutes their irreducible *dieresis*: "insofar as this intuition cannot be compared to a universal geometrical figure but is particular to each soul like a perception of light in each eye; it is here a merely individual revelation; however, in this individuality there is also a universal revelation, just as light is for the empirical senses" (Schelling 1989, p. 15).

Far from subsuming the singularity of phenomena under the *logos* of the concept, Schelling's Platonism rather attempts to salvage phenomena from their reduction to attributes, predicates and numbers. Essences of phenomena are neither facts nor concepts but their truth. [3] As un-subsumable and un-subsuming archetypes, ideas are potencies or potentialities of the absolute, forms of determination in which absolute appears as *singular-universal.* Such an idea of truth cannot be conceived within the categorical-cognitive-predicative structure of judgment. The universality of ideas is absolved from genus, since the universality of ideas here is not achieved in the conceptual manner of subsumption. The harmony of these ideas, which Schelling compares with the constellation of celestial bodies, is here the image of a happiness unimpaired by the violence of cognitive enclosures[4]. Each of the potencies in its unique, singular and un-subsumable mode is at once a singular reflection of the absolute as a whole; each exhibit, in its own manner, its own time at conjunction with eternity, its mortality with immortality, its limitation with the immeasurable. In their irreducible singularity, ideas are super-numeric: they can neither be measured by numbers, nor can they be determined by attributes, nor they can be assigned to any denomination by given predicates of a subject. "For just this reason", writes Schelling, "all number or determination by number is suspended. The particular [singular] thing in absoluteness is not determined by number, for if one reflects upon the particular within it, it is itself the absolute whole and possesses nothing outside of or external to itself. If one reflects upon the universal, it is in absolute unity with all other things. Accordingly, only it itself subsumes or comprehends unity and multiplicity within itself, though it is itself not capable of being determined by these concepts" (Schelling 1989, p. 34).

Potencies are nondescript singularities like life. The absolute operates here unsuffocated by the plethora of attributes, numbers, and predicates. The freedom that ideas enjoy in this state of blessedness also constitutes the very enigma of life: "life is found only within particularity [singularity]" (Ibid., pp. 36-7). Unlike the violence of theoretical cognition that subordinates singularity to an empty generality, it is the task of philosophical-intellectual intuition to redeem singularities from their reduction and totalization into logic of objects (of cognition). Such redemption from the violence of cognition makes possible their participation in the divine excess and that releases them to the unconditional blessedness or absolute beatitude. As singulars, "they nonetheless enjoy the blessedness of the absolute, and vice versa (to strive toward blessedness= to strive as a particular [singular] to partake of absoluteness)" (Ibid., p. 39).

Art, philosophy and religion: these are three modes of partaking of the unconditional, the three modes of absolute beatitude which is the highest possibility of existence *arriving* to us. Schelling conceives the idea of beatitude eschatologically. The unconditional beatitude is the eschatological arrival in-excess of all measurement of numbers, of all predications and judgments, of all qualifying attributes of a cognitive "object". Appearing as harmony, as in the harmony of celestial bodies, beatitude is the task of philosophical contemplation and presentation of their truth. Such blessedness is an unsaturated gift coming from an eschatological excess which is the excess of eternity over time.[5] To participate in this eschatological possibility, philosophy must assume the task of mortification, that of releasing the soul of phenomena from its enclosure into their brute empirical existence. The truth of phenomenon which is none but absolute beauty must be released, through mortification, from its subsumption to the law of conditionality. In other words, attributes, predicates and numbers by which the work of subsumption is made possible, must undergo their mortification so that the unconditional may be presented *as* unconditional. Such philosophical work of mortification, far from wounding phenomenon with violence of subsumption, redeems it and thereby enables it to participate in the radiance of absolute beatitude.

Despite Schelling's infamous restlessness which inhabits and unworks all his attempts to constitute a definitive "system", I would like to argue that Schelling has remained singularly attuned to the fundamental philosophical task of his life that he articulates in this series of lectures on the philosophy of art. This task consists of releasing the eschatological potentiality of the unconditional from all possible enclosures of the immanence of conditional self-presence. This, in turn, demands from us a work of mortification to operate on attributes, predicates and numbers so that truth and beauty of phenomena present themselves in their unsaturated excess, now freed from these normative enclosures and referents that constitute them into "objects" of rational cognition.

II. Allegory of the Invisible

Schelling's 1802-3 series of lectures on the philosophy of art begins with a historical presentation of two successive conceptions of the relation of infinite and finite, the universal and the singular, the unconditional and conditioned. Instead of conceiving various works of art from different historical periods under common, generalizing concepts, Schelling presents a historical construction of the content of art. The content of art is said to be "mythological" whose meaning Schelling deduces in the course of his investigation. Thus the Greek mode of presentation is understood to be symbolic (which is a synthesis of schematic and allegorical)[6], a realist mythology in which the synthesis of finite and infinite is achieved in such a way that the finite counts in itself without being subsumed in the infinite. In the symbolic representation of the realist mythology the wedding of the infinite and finite is presented as their *simultaneity* as in a constellation of celestial bodies where the infinite radiates itself in each finite body. This space of simultaneity in which each symbol is unique and singular at the same time is the space of nature. This symbolic world of nature can be said to exist without history in the sense that it has not yet fallen into time, into succession of potencies. Necessity is felt here as fate that Greek tragedies represent symbolically on the stage of theatre. These ideas are nothing other than archetypes with which mythology, as its content, is "properly" concerned with[7]. In this sense, mythology is the content of Greek works of art (and of philosophy) as such. Nature here is the tragic stage where the individual is not yet experienced as separated from the collective, the finite is not yet felt apart from the infinite, "where the highest morality lies in the recognition of the boundaries and limitations to which human beings are subject" (Ibid., p. 55). The simultaneity of beings belonging together as archetypes enables us to conceive the philosophical polytheism as the proper possibility of Greek mythology. The rebellion of the finite against the infinite conjures up fate but since the finite is not just to be annihilated for the sake of the infinite, this rebellion marks the very heroic virtues and sublimity of the tragic people of Greece.

The decay of this mythological content has brought to an end the epoch of the Greek antiquity. Taking birth on the ruin of the tragic stage of Greek nature, Christianity brings into the stage of existence, not nature but history, not mythology but allegory, not infinite at one with the finite but infinite that is removed to a transcendence without measure: "Mythology concludes as soon as allegory begins" (Ibid., p. 48). Schelling cites the fall of the Roman Empire as the most remarkable moment of this rupture between the decay of the mythological world and the birth of the allegorical. The decadence of the Roman Empire has brought dissatisfaction with the immanence of mythic existence. The infinite now no longer is experienced as immanent within the well-rounded sphere of mythic nature but is removed to the furthest, to an unattainable beyond of nature. The immanence of mythic continuity where figures of the divine immediately manifest themselves on the stage of nature is no longer felt sufficient. It is now replaced by a succession of historical epochs that partially disclose a God otherwise hidden from nature. The absconding infinite renders impossible satisfaction of the human spirit in the immanent mode of mythic existence. Schelling marks this moment as the birth of modernity. The dissatisfied modern man now wrests himself loose, almost violently, from the satisfaction in laws of the earth and in the fruits of its soil.

> The modern world begins when man wrests himself loose from nature. Since he does not yet have a new home, however, he feels abandoned. Wherever such a feeling comes over an entire group, that group turns either voluntarily or compelled by an inner urge to the ideal world in order to find a home. Such a feeling had come over the world when Christianity arose. Greece's beauty was gone; Rome, which has collected all the world's splendour into itself, lay crushed under its own massive weight. The complete saturation and satisfaction of all objective needs naturally generated boredom and an inclination towards the element of the ideal... the universal feeling that a new world must come, since the old one was no longer able to continue, lay like sultry air over the entire world at that time, an atmosphere like that announcing a great movement in nature (Ibid., pp. 59-60).

The birth of history renders nature non-autochthonous, bereft of any inherent meaning and beauty. No longer fate but providence is now experienced in this tragic stage of history[8]. Uprooted from its mythic immanence and exposed to an immeasurable boundlessness in all sides, man himself becomes the separated being, spaced between nature and history, time and eternity, individual and the collective, finite and the infinite. In such a condition of worldlessness and homelessness[9], infinite can be presented not as simultaneous with finite but only as succession, as an utter transient manifestation like the flickering of a light appearing against an immense abyss of darkness, only to be momentarily held fast. While the infinite has now absconded to an indeterminate and un-localizable place which is a "non-place", the finite too has lost its inherent meaningfulness and its innermost validity. Deprived of both the infinite and finite, the abandoned man looks for the unity of being, now sundered apart, in an eschatological future. Schelling conceives this eschatological future in terms of a mythology, not the mythology of mythic immanence whose glory is now past but a mythology *to come*. The loss of archetypes, marking the decay of mythology which is Greek (for, properly speaking, mythology is Greek), opens now for the first time the birth of religion. Schelling then, strictly speaking does not understand the tragic world of Greek mythology to have religion at all, for religion is a historical phenomenon, incommensurable with the mythic context of Greek consciousness. Religion is rather a negation and replacement of mythology. The Gnostic Schelling here—and we will have more to say on this aspect of Schelling—conceives religion as homelessness that tirelessly attempts to unbind man from the cages of the world as it exists. Religion, writes Schelling,

> ...necessarily assumes the character of a revealed religion and is for that reason historical at its very foundation. Greek religion, as a poetic religion living through the collectively itself, had no need of a historical foundation, as little as does nature, which is always open. The manifestations and figures of the gods here were eternal. In Christianity, on the other hand, the divine was only a fleeting appearance and had to be held fast in this appearance (Schelling 1989, p. 69).

In the tragic-mythic unity of beings, nature is *always already* open. In this Open of nature, the divine manifestations are eternal, enduring presence. Nature is the landscape of blazing clarity where Gods appear in their pure immanence. On the other hand, in the tragic-religious absolute disunion of the infinite and the finite, nature is withdrawn as mystery. The opening of the finite to the infinite can now only be conceived as that which "falls into time and accordingly from history". "For this reason Christianity in its innermost spirit and highest sense is historical. Every particular moment of time is a revelation of a particular side of God, and in each he is absolute. What Greek religion possessed as simultaneity, Christianity possesses as succession even if the time of separation of appearances and with it of form has not yet come" (Ibid., p. 63).

Schelling, then, conceives religion as the historical phenomenon par excellence. The concept of revelation, as philosophical necessity, presupposes not the mythic context of continuity but the historical disjunction between the phenomenal realm and the wholly other, freed from laws of the profane order. As revelation as its intrinsic principle, religion disrupts the serenity of the mythic immanence and introduces into the world the abyss of an absolute caesura between the infinite and finite, collective and individual, nature and history, transcendence and immanence. The synthesis of infinite and finite, now no longer being available as archetypes as they were in the mythic context of nature, makes symbolic representation impossible. Thus the displacement of the mythic context by the absolute disunion of religion has its counterpart in the artistic modes of representation: symbolic representation of archetypes is being displaced by the allegorical mode of representation. While mythology is symbolism of the finite which in itself is at one with the infinite, religion on the other hand is an allegory of the infinite. In such an allegorical mode of representation, the finite is emptied of its inherent signification and the infinite is removed to an inaccessible transcendence beyond nature. On this stage of history, the infinite or the divine may appear only in its utter weakness, like that of Christ dying an ignoble death on the cross of history[10]. Like a flickering light against an immense, unfathomable darkness of the night, the logic of manifestation of the divine on the profane order does not follow the determinate order of necessity, unlike the determinate order of mythic immanence marked by fate. Schelling's metaphor here is that of the sudden appearance of the comet, a transient apparition in this desolate landscape of Christianity. Its incalculable apparition sets the worldlessness of Christianity in remarkable contrast to the metaphor of the eternal harmony of the planets which is the symbolic-mythic space of Greek blessedness,

> The ancients are the planets of the world of art, limited to a few individuals who are simultaneously the collective and who nonetheless even in the highest freedom of movement remove themselves the least from their identity with that collective. Taken as a group themselves, these planet analogies are also characterized by definite subtypes. Those with the most depth are the rhythmic ones. Those more distant—where the mass structures itself as a totality, where everything positions itself concentrically in rings and moons around the centre, like the petals of a blossom—are the dramatic ones. Boundless space belongs to the comets. When they appear, they come directly from infinite space, and though they well may draw near to the sun, just as certainly do they also distance themselves from it again (Ibid., p. 74).

In this metaphor of the comet Schelling presents an allegory of the infinite which is the phenomenon *absconditus* par excellence. Even the appearance of Christ on the stage of history does not make the world any more "homely" for the fallen mankind. Here the meaning of the infinite is not presented as an enduring and eternal presence fixed in their mythic blessedness, but a transiency that must be wrested at opportune, incalculable moments as soon as it appears momentarily against a boundless darkness of non-being. Thinking in the manner of Pauline eschatology in which Gnosticism of the early Christianity was still resonating, Schelling presents [11]these moments as *turns of time* (*Kairos*). The infinite reveals itself at these turnings of time allegorically, that is, without being exhaustively determined by the determinate logic of historical Reason. Religion for Schelling is none other than this *Kairos* allegory of revelation. In the manner that the law of the comet's appearance cannot be subsumed under the homogeneous logic of the conceptual-historical Reason, so the allegory of the infinite cannot be grasped on the basis of the symbolic representation of archetypes. Religion thus exceeds both the mythic context of nature which is ruled by the law of eternal recurrence of the same and that of historical Reason that presents the whole of historical order itself under the law of quantitative and homogeneous process of Reason's self-becoming.

This last point is of utmost importance for us. Schelling's eschatological deconstruction sets itself against the immanent order of mythic immanence as well against the historical Reason which consolidates itself in Schelling's own time. Religion is neither "natural" nor simply "historical" (at least in the sense determined by historical Reason of the 19th century). The new sense of religion given to us by Schelling is "eschatological". It too is historical, but in a wholly other sense. Religion in this new sense is the non-originary, non-autarchic and non-sovereign opening to the infinite; religion as an incessant and adamant opening to an excess beyond all enclosures of mythic immanence and beyond the self-sufficiency of the laws of the earth. Far from sinking its teeth in the *nomos* of the earth, and thereby finding consolation in the self-satisfaction with what already exists, religion opens itself to an eschatological arrival which is disjointed from what already exists in the profane realm of world-domination.

Thus allegory of religion, in itself indeterminate of meaning and emptied of all inherent self-foundation, is the very opening up of meaning, now no longer exhausted in the language of judgment and predication. It is this irreducible anguish of disjointure, this absolute suffering of disunion, and this utter desolation of a caesura is what Schelling calls "religion". It is not "re"-ligion in the sense of re-binding to the *nomos* of the earth but an eschatological un-binding, an antinomic releasing open to a future mythology to arrive. At the very heart of the mythic unity of being, religion opens up an abyss of exodus wherein the divine can present itself only as absconding.[12]The uncoupling of religion from the mythic immanence introduces a disruption, a separation or a caesura within the realm of Christianity itself. Unlike the Greek symbolic order which does not need to have a historical foundation and wherein its "religion" exists inseparable from the state, in Christianity, on the other hand, "there is a separate history of religion and of the Church" (Schelling 1989, p. 69). Christianity for Schelling, in its very spirit and promise and from its very inception, is a religion of separation and partitioning of the modes of being. By virtue of being given in such an indelible wound of caesura, it is set apart from politics, as if as it were, each having a history of its own from the other, separated by an irreducible abyss of meaning, by an empty space of time.

The question of the miracle here is particularly revealing. The possibility of a miracle, like the appearance of the comet, is only possible in Christianity and not in the mythic context of nature. This is because the occurrence of a miracle presupposes the possibility of absolute and incalculable disunion, of the un-binding of the law of the earth and of the dismemberment of infinite and finite. Schelling can, thus, say: "Christianity, which is possible only within absolute disunion, is at its very inception already founded on miracles. A miracle is an absolute viewed from the empirical perspective, an absolute occurring within the finite realm without for that reason having any relationship to time "(Ibid., p. 69).

Religion as such and Christianity in particular would mean for Schelling none other than the instance of "setting apart". This fundamental cision (*Scheidung*) or, this un-binding must release the eschatological potentiality of the future from the foundation of the world. Such eschatological potentiality constantly opens the closures of history to a future mythology *to* arrive. In Schellingian terms, Christianity is to be understood in this verbal resonance of the infinitive "to". Such eschatology, which is the principle of religion in a fundamental sense, is absolutely incommensurable to the mythic world of immanence. The eschatological suffering, insofar as the world as it exists is perceived to be insufficient, understands the potencies or powers of the world claiming sovereignty to be insufficient, being transient and null of any inherent signification and validity. Even though the church is the only symbolic body within Christianity that bears the character of public manifestation, even it cannot claim absolute obligation from us insofar as the reason of its very being is separate from that of the state.

In the antinomic eschatological schema of Schellingian thought, religion manifests in the world as an inoperation of political sovereignty that already exists. When the sting of such inoperation is taken away from religion, it becomes not only like any other powers that manifests in the profane realm of world-domination but becomes their very foundation. In more than one place, Schelling asks us to beware of dangers that arise from the acts of political legitimization on a theological foundation. Even Christianity as it exists, insofar as it exists as non-absolute, can only be for Schelling a transition (in its verbal infinitive "to") to a future mythology. Such final destiny of mankind demands, however, that we pass through the entire eschatological passage of history to a fulfilment (*pleroma*) always to come, an arrival which is not grasped in the self-generating concept of reason as in Hegel, but is intimated in the prophetic waiting for *pleroma* to burst into the stage of history.

III. Breaking-Away

It is of singular importance that in Schellingian eschatology, the ethical is always thought to be irreducible to the political. As "a directive for beatific life" (Schelling 2010, p. 8) ethics is seen to be the surplus of politics, if the political is to be understood as the realm of conditioned negotiations and pragmatic engagement with the sovereign powers of the world[13]. Beatitude on the other hand, which is the unconditional principle at one with truth, cannot be attained by the powers of the world-historical orders. The ethical here is neither understood in terms of the Kantian regulative-formal principle of moral law nor in terms of the Hegelian notion of absolute concept but as the exuberance of a life opening to the unconditional *eschaton* of beatitude. This is because the Kantian mere-formal regulative principle of moral law appears to Schelling to be an empty experience bereft the historical and linguistic constituents of our exuberant existence. Similarly the Hegelian dialectical negative philosophy, in its reduction of "the riddle of existence" to the webs of the conceptual order, works like legitimacy seeking political order of the state machinery which, by its works of law, attempts to reduce life into a mere functionary of the state. Schelling thinks *life* itself eschatologically, oriented to the absolute beatitude which must be released both from the cages of the *nomos* of world-domination and from its petrification into the formal order of an inherently empty experience. The ethical here is not just a part of a composite existence which can be added and subtracted at will, but rather is the very apex, the summit of life which is a non-composite and nondescript singular-whole. Life as a whole must orient itself towards this absolute beatitude, towards this nameless Good and not a part of life which is "ethical" or "political". Such "towardness" of life in its entirety follows a logic heterogeneous to the law of calculable economy, a logic unthinkable in the categorical mode of rational cognition.

In his 1804 *Philosophy and Religion,* Schelling tentatively works towards an expression of such metaphysics of life. Life is not a composite; it is neither a product nor result of the unification of opposites (subjective and objective) nor an object of rational cognition attained through negative descriptions. The singularity of such life which is simultaneously universal is nondescript, indemonstrable and unexplainable, for "only a composite can be known through description" (Schelling 2010, p. 15). Only intellectual intuition can open itself to the indemonstrable disclosure of the non-composite absolute. Life, being finite, is its weak eschatological reflection. The germ of Schelling's future Hegel-critique already is seen here even before Hegel's critique of Schelling coming on the philosophical scene. For such intellectual intuition of life as a whole, the categorical-cognitive and negative descriptions of the absolute are never final. This is because such negative descriptions must already presuppose an affirmation before all negativity of description, demonstration and production. One cannot miss in the following lines, clearly inspired by Meister Eckhart and Plato, that the future Hegelian critique is already anticipated by Schelling:

> For as the essence of God consists of absolute, solely unmediated reality, so the nature of the soul consists in cognition that is one with the real, ergo with God; hence it is also the intention of philosophy in relation to man not to add anything but to remove from him, as thoroughly as possible, the accidentals that the body, the world of appearances, and the sensate life have added and to lead him back to the originary state. Furthermore, all instruction in philosophy that precedes this cognition can only be negative; it shows the nullity of all finite opposites and leads the soul indirectly to the perception of the infinite. Once there, it is no longer in need of those makeshift devices of negative descriptions of absoluteness and sets itself free from them (Ibid).

Schellingian metaphysics of life expresses itself in an indemonstrable excess of affirmation, a *Yes* before all, a Yes "before" that cannot be traced back apophantically or through syllogistic forms of rational cognition. [14] It is as if an abyss *sets apart* the unconditional affirmation of beatitude from all possible negative descriptions that regressively want to return to the "originary state". Between the ethical orientation of life to the absolute beatitude (which is to be unconditionally) affirmed and the systematic order achieved through the negative work of the concept there lies an abyss of *breaking away*. If Hegel understood the state as one of the highest expressions or "one of the figures of the negative" (Wirth 2003, p. 22), then the ethical demand of the unconditional would not find satisfaction with the happiness that man attains in the profane order of the political. Schelling thus perceives the state less as the glorifying figure of the absolute but that which belongs to the realm of apostasy (*Abfall*) even in its highest expression, a mere symptom of the fundamental disjunction or the fall from the absolute.

What Schelling calls here in the manner of Meister Eckhart and Plato as "the originary state" where the like is recognized by the like[15], is never an "origin" in this sense. Here is not a homogeneous, continuous line through which one reaches back, in a retrogressive manner, to the point of a mythic origin lying at the very beginning (which, retrogressively, is the end) of that line. "The originary state" is rather to be understood as an eschatological arrival from the extremity of the future that disrupts the immanence of any mythic origin. "The originary state" is an immemorial past *to come* from an eschatological future, that is, by *breaking away* from the mythic immanence of a creationism as well as from the logic of emanation and continuum, as if a re-turn to the originary is only possible on the basis of a fundamental experience of *distance* or apartness from origin at all. Eschatology in that sense cannot be understood mythically but as the fundamental opening of re-ligion, religion that re-turns to the originary without returning to the origin, wherein originary *breaks away* from the origin, wherein the originary is yet to be disclosed in the extremity of time *to* come. The "originary" without "origin" is the meaning of *eschaton* and of religion, meaning of a "to" in its irreducible verbal resonance of the infinitive.

Schelling's 1804 essay is a remarkable document. Perhaps this is Schelling's first attempt at a renewal of metaphysics that seriously incorporates the idea of falling away or breaking away (*Abfall*), an idea that is to find such utmost intensity of expression in his 1809 treatise on human freedom. Schelling scholars rightly point out here the influence of Jacob Böhme. What is fascinating in this context is Schelling's deduction of the problem of the political on the basis of this metaphysical framework of *breaking away*, a framework that enables Schelling to think of the political as the realm that cannot claim the legitimacy of its sovereignty insofar as the realm of the political, by virtue of its non-autochthony and non-autarchy, must de-legitimize itself out of its very ontological possibility.

How that ontological possibility of the political is understood in Schellingian metaphysics in such a way that the revolutionary potentialities of the *eschaton* is released from its enclosures in the mythic immanence of self-presence? If the essential content of this discourse called "philosophy" must be understood as none other than "the eternal birth of all things and their relationship to God" (Ibid., p. 8), then philosophy as metaphysics must account, without recourse to blind faith or irrational premonitions of any type, such birth "of all things". Metaphysics must account for the potencies or potentialities of all things. Metaphysics as such is a discourse of potentiality. First worked out in his *Philosophy of Nature*, Schelling presents here the theory of potencies that must be able to give an account of how difference, the essential condition of all finite, phenomenal mode of being, erupts out of the Absolute which Schelling at that time understood it as the absolute principle of identity.

The dominant metaphysics of the Occident explains the event of the eruption of difference and consequently the birth of the phenomenal world on the model of emanation and creation. The phenomenal world of difference is grasped as gradual decrement from the light of the origin, the progressive darkening and opaqueness of being to the point in which the clarity of the origin is submerged in the abyss of non-being, this non-being in turn is determined to be matter. The metaphysical model of the dominant metaphysics of the Occident is that of continuity: a homogeneous, quantitative, progressively downward line connects the clarity of the origin with the most debased and the most abject phenomenon called evil. It is in the Neo-Platonic conception of emanation wherein this dominant metaphysics of continuity finds its definitive expression. The dominant metaphysics of the Occident is thus onto-theo-logically constituted: the God as the ground of beings, as the sovereign origin of all phenomenality or as Absolute concept that includes within it the entire history of the concept's self-becoming (Hegel). From

Plotinus to Hegel, including Leibniz, the framework of continuity, with its ideas of emanation and creation, has remained the sovereign metaphysical framework, the ultimate ontological horizon in the West. Religion is understood as "re-legion": binding back to the mythic origin. Religion in its revolutionary potentiality and in its eschatological energy is replaced with a theology of creation or a theodicy of history as in Hegelian historical-speculative dialectics. Such theodicy of history founded upon the notions of creation and emanation is pantheism in its most fulfilled expression. The divine is claimed to be embodied, even if in a privative manner, on the profane realm of the world-historical politics. The unjustifiable violence and evil of the world-historical politics can here be justified as necessary privation of the Good. Evil appears as a mere attenuated variation of the universal march of history whose continuity is constantly being filled up with events falling as into an empty scale of time. The historical Reason of 19th century Europe, arising out of and against Enlightenment, ends up being an apologist of what exists, since what already exists appears inevitable and necessary, given the continuity of the line that necessarily connects the clarity of the origin and the fulfilment of it at its end.

Schelling's 1804 essay can now be seen, retrospectively, as one of the first decisive ruptures into the history of philosophy, opening metaphysics itself to a wholly new inauguration of thinking that anticipates Marx, Kierkegaard and Nietzsche. With it the history of the Occidental metaphysics itself momentarily comes to a caesura. By introducing the revolutionary potentiality of eschatological thinking into philosophical discourse and thereby breaking away from the creation-theology of Pantheism and from the theodicy of historical Reason, Schelling's theory of potencies opens itself to the thought of radical finitude and what is considered to be the scandal of metaphysics, that is, the question of radical evil.

This essay *Philosophy and Religion* undertakes the task of deconstruction of the dominant metaphysics of the Occident by posing the unthought and the scandalous question of traditional metaphysics: the possibility and actuality of the radical evil. If the radical evil cannot be seen to have derived directly from God (that will make him the originator of evil), this possibility and actuality of evil exposes the metaphysics of emanation and creation to its aporia, for the possibility and actuality of radical evil presupposes a radical disjunction or discontinuity, a fundamental *breaking away* or *falling away* in the very nexus of beings, an idea unthinkable in the traditional philosophy of emanation. For the radical evil to be possible, or even for the phenomenal order to be possible at all, the abyss of a separation or distance must occur between the Absolute and the finite-phenomenal order. An immeasurable distance, an interval breaking the circle of mythic immanence, a distressful separation inhabits all Pantheistic attempts at analogy and continuity between the divine and the profane order. Schelling writes,

> ...[I]n the absolute world there are no confines anywhere, and just as God can only bring forth the real-per-se and absolute, so any ensuing effulgence is again absolute and can itself only bring forth something akin to it. There can be no continuous passage into the exact opposite, the absolute privation of all reality, nor can the finite arise from the infinite by decrements (Ibid., p. 24).

The idea of continuity cannot explain the birth of the phenomenal world. It can only be conceivable as *falling away* or breaking away from the Absolute "by means of a leap",

> If philosophy were able to derive the origin of the actual world in a positive manner from the Absolute, then the Absolute would have its positive cause in the same; however, in God resides only the cause of the ideas, and only those produce other ideas. There is no positive effect coming out of the Absolute that creates a conduit or bridge between the infinite and finite. Furthermore: philosophy has only a negative relation to phenomenal objects; since it demonstrates less the truth of their being than their non-being, how could it therefore ascribe to them a positive relationship to God? The absolute is the only actual; the finite world, by contrast, is not real. Its cause, therefore, cannot lie in an impartation of reality from the Absolute to the finite world or its substrate; it can only lie in a *remove*, in a *falling away* from the Absolute" (Ibid., 26).

"Remove" or "falling away" (*Abfall*) is the fundamental eschatological principle of Schelling. Reading Plato against the dominant understanding of the Neo-Platonic idea of emanation and against the creation theology of Christianity, Schelling deconstructs the dominant onto-theology of the West[16]. It is as if, as it were, a removal, a distance, a falling away must first open up a space of abyss (*Abgrund*) in order for the phenomenal world to take birth. What would this space of abyss be if it were not the abyss of freedom? The birth of the world arises in this abyss of freedom whose essence is a non-being[17]. It is this non-being, this finite self-hood of freedom, separated from the Absolute in its self-dependence, that *potentiates* the world and not Absolute in-itself directly. Actuality of the world, however, lies in the *falling away* itself. With this, Schelling's eschatology turns creation-theology inside out. The ground, the cause, the foundation of the phenomenal world cannot now be traced back to the Absolute directly but only to the abyss of a freedom that is the counter-image of the Absolute. Like Meister Eckhart's Godhead beyond even God, the Schellingian Absolute too cannot even be called a principle, an arché, a sovereign cause, as original foundation of the phenomenal order. This Absolute is not even potentiality but actuality without potentiality, a *non-arché*, a non-sovereign Good before the distinction that comes to be with the fall of man, the distinction between good and evil.

The idea of the soul that Schelling adopts here is the Gnostic-Cabbalistic principle of *Pneuma*. It is the remainder of that divine sparkle that is left over in the fallen world, the remnant of a light that is now imprisoned in the cages of law. It is the acosmic, "ahistorical", spectral Gnostic principle, now eschatologically conceived by Schelling, which must be released from the cages of the world-historical order of earthly sovereignty. The soul here is the other principle, otherwise than a "principle": worldless, independent of time, a dim reflection of the absolute. Rather than bearing the positive knowledge of the phenomenal order, it rather bears witness the nonbeing of all that is earthly, including the powerful regimes of the world-historical politics. This eschatological *Pneuma*, by virtue of its discontinuous relation to the *nomos* of the world, does not have its equivalence in the external, conditioned relationships of the worldly existence. The absolute breaking away from the Absolute undoes all attempts to embody the divine on the domain of the world-historical politics on the basis of analogy. "No fine thing can directly originate from the Absolute or be traced back to it", Schelling says, "whereby the cause of the finite world is expressed as an absolute breaking away from the infinite world" (Ibid., p. 29).

Schelling, therefore, does not see the possibility of partaking in the gift of the absolute beatitude in a direct mode. The influence of Meister Eckhart here is unmistakable again: partaking in the gift of beatitude demands an indirection which is mortification of all egotism and releasement of *Pneuma* from its imprisonment in the *nomos* of the worldly-sensate life. If the fundamental presupposition of Pantheism is the idea that the phenomenal worldly order has its inherent, positive being of its own, then Schelling's self-understanding of his own philosophy, which is based upon an irreducible separation, doesn't allow Pantheism as the appropriate designation of his philosophy (Ibid., pp. 37-38). The inescapable remainder of the rift, or cleft, opened in the very opening of the world to itself, will forever haunt any theologico-political totalization of our existence. Rather than closing the abyss here by the force of worldly powers of sovereignty, Schelling thinks here of a path of indirection, that is, intensification of the separation as the very releasing open to the absolute beatitude. What it calls forth from us is an infinite task of mortification or renunciation of the world-historical claim to sovereignty. When such mortification occurs, and when the abyss of separation in its distress is not congealed in the *nomos* of world-historical powers but is released open to its very distress, the surprise of beatitude arrives without condition. Schelling considers the unconditional arrival of beatitude as inseparable from the highest morality, not the morality which we must succumb "like single bodies succumb to gravity" (Ibid., p. 43), but more like the blessed celestial bodies wherein the polarity of two paths—egress and return, centrifugal and centripetal—coincide, not just accidentally but in an essential manner. The metaphor of the celestial body once again enables Schelling to conceive the blessedness of this mode of being wherein polarity of two paths coincide[18],

> Just as an idea—and its reflection, the celestial body—absorbs its center, identity, and at once resides within it, and vice-versa, so also the soul; it's inclination toward the center, to be one with God, is morality. This would only be a negative difference, were it not for the fact that the resumption finitude into infinitude is also a passage of the infinite into the finite, e.g. a complete being—within-itself of the latter. Thus morality and beatitude are but two different sides of the same oneness; in no need of being complemented by the other, each is absolute and comprehends the other. The originary image of being-one which is that of both truth and beauty is God (Schelling 2010, p. 43).

Nature is "the image of God's beatitude" (Ibid., p. 44). What is a celestial body in the realm of nature, in the eschatological conception of the history it is the coincidence of freedom and necessity. In the realm of the ethical, it is to be understood as the coincidence of truth and beauty, virtue and beatitude[19].

As primarily ethical, wherein ethical is understood as "direction to a beatific life" (Ibid., p. 8), Schelling conceives religion that can only have an indirect relation to the order of the political. Even in its highest moral order, the state cannot be seen as an embodiment of the divine. Distinguishing within religion itself its esoteric and exoteric dimensions, its secret mystery cult and its public-external form, religion can only have the meaning of *secrecy.* Thus writes Schelling: "God, however, as identity of the highest order, remains above all reality and eternally has merely an indirect relationship. If then in the higher moral order the state represents a *second nature*, then the divine can never have anything other than an indirect relationship to it; never can it bear any real relationship to it, and religion, if it seeks to preserve itself in unscathed pure ideality, can therefore never exist—even in the most perfect state—other than esoterically in the form of *mystery cults*" (Ibid., 51). Withdrawn from all public and private manifestation, religion does not have its home in the significance of world-historical manifestation. Neither public nor private, neither external nor mere interiority, religion is *secret* in an essential sense: secrecy as withdrawal from the meaningful order of the world-political manifestation, a withdrawal of an immemorial language from the linguistic registrar of judgment and signification. In Schellingian eschatology, the triumphal order of the world-historical politics is thus stripped of the final significance. The "last disclosure" (Ibid., p. 55) which will reconcile the "the falling away from the Absolute" and transform this negativity into an unconditional affirmation, would rather exhibit the nullity of all such triumphalism of the order of the world-historical politics. History is predicated upon freedom and not vice-versa. "Thus, religion", writes Schelling, "having a purely moral effect, is kept from the danger of mixing with the real, the sensate, or from laying claims to external dominion and violence, which would be contrary to its nature. Philosophy, on the other hand, and those enamoured with it, the naturally initiated, remain eternally allied with religion" (Ibid.).

IV. Schelling's Ontology of Separation

In his 1810 private lectures at Stuttgart, Schelling brings further intensification and concretion into his earlier conception of caesura or separation. The influence of Jacob Böhme, already manifest in his freedom essay, passes through these lectures and finds it's most profound and creative expression in his incomplete *The Ages of the World.* The notion of "transition" from essence to existence and from potentiality into actuality is grasped here, in the manner of Böhme, not on the basis of the principle of continuity and emanation but as the most fundamental crisis of "caesura" (*Scheidung*) that enables revelation *Offenbarung*) to break through as divine life. This *setting apart* of *transition* is less a cancellation of identity but the *doubling* (*Doublirung*) of essence that rends asunder the polar principles of the divine being (and so of the mortal being). What Being (*Seyn*) is to being (*das Seyende*), that the foundation to existence. The former, being mere foundation, serves as the non-being to the latter while still having a being of its own, an independent life, self-hood of its own[20]. In fact, it is this non-being that is the principle of self-hood, the principle of finitude and negativity. In contrast to Hegel's *Logic* (who does not distinguish non-being from nothingness), Schelling distinguishes this principle of non-being (which Being –*Seyn* - is) from "nothingness". The latter cannot be said to be the principle of freedom, for only as the non-being of freedom can there be finitude, self-hood, personality and actuality. A philosophy of freedom like that of Schelling's cannot begin with the concept of nothingness that passes into being and vice-versa[21] but only with the non-being as the potentiality of being (*das Seyende*). That is why there always remains a residue of non-being, an irreducible remainder, a remnant of darkness, even when it is actualized and elevated into the light of being (*das Seyende*). The eternal remnant of non-being, as the very condition of possibility of life, thus refuses the Hegelian *Aufhebung* into the Absolute concept as something that eternally falls outside "being" and outside the thinkable.

Against the Neo-Platonic conception of emanation as against the Hegelian pantheistic theodicy of history, the eschatology of Schelling makes this "principle" of separation as the very condition of existence and actuality, of life and revelation. God contracts, limits, withdraws, restricts or descends himself[22] by virtue of his absolute freedom[23], bringing into being the absolute crisis of separation between principles, expelling (without thereby extinguishing) the principle of self-hood into the dark, abyssal foundation of being[24] . Difference thus opened by this crisis of separation and by partitioning for powers is the non-axiological difference, not difference grasped as a succession of conceptual categories as in Hegel but difference as *holding*-together (*Zusammenhang*) that Schelling conceives as "simultaneity"[25]. Such difference is not a mere attenuated variation of identity but difference *as* difference, for only as the non-axiological difference can the phenomenal realm of the world and mortal can still have a relative self-dependence of being apart from God[26]. Gilles Deleuze rightly perceives in this Schellingian ontology of separation a decisive attempt to think difference *as* difference irreducible to the representation of difference.[27] Life can only be found in this *apartness* opened by the abyss of difference, in this partitioning of powers, in this *parting away* of ground and existence. Such life, actualized and exuberant and not a mere logical category can only exist as bond, as nexus, as jointure among beings: God, man and nature in which man is the intermediary link, the point of transition between God and nature.

Man appears in such an ontological nexus of beings as the condition of continuity of beings, continuity that is *always already* opened in the abyss of discontinuity emerging from the night of indifference. As "transition" (which is in fact a "rupture") from God to nature, man is simultaneously *removed*, separated, parted from both God and nature.[28] This means: an essential disjointure must always already operate as potentiality in the very jointure and continuity that runs from God to nature through the historical passage of man in this world. In this drama of redemption occurring on this stage of history, the place or rather the non-place of man is the crucial hinge. As the hinge which may open as well as close beings towards redemption, as the hinge that is potentiality of both continuity and discontinuity and of both jointure and disjointure of beings, man must duplicate the very crisis of separation of principles in himself on the basis of his freedom borrowed from the absolute freedom of God. Like God, he too must separate in his own finite realm the dark, unconscious principle from the ideal principle of light in order to constantly elevate the expelled principle into the light of revelation.

Such ontology of separation is at the same time an ontology of strife, grounded in the groundless (*Abgrund*) freedom. As the fundamental law of opposition and strife constitutes the very life of the divine, so the same opposition and strife rules within the finite life of the mortal. The continuity of beings, arising out of the fundamental cision of principles, cannot therefore be a homogeneous line of progressive succession. Released from the logic of "progressivity" (Deleuze 1994, p. 191) which is the image of thought that understands difference on the basis of the identical, the jointure of beings can be disjointed[29], the nexus can be broken, the bond can undergo displacement, and the continuity of beings can be disrupted, since it arises out of the groundless freedom. Man as the linkage in this continuity of beings can also be the very condition of their discontinuity when there occurs inversion of principles in him, when the non-being in its incessant hunger for being attempts to assume the place of being (*das Seyende*).Evil is thereby let loose on the spiritual stage of history, the passage of communication and continuity among beings undergoes clotting (*Stockung*) or inhibition (*Hemmung*)[30], affecting the entire connection that he has with God and nature. Cut off from man because of his fault and from partaking of divine life, nature now sees no more in man her redemptive possibility. She suffers the most unspeakable of diseases. Man too, now finding no way to relate to God and nature, suffers the most violent disease of spirit. The disease in nature finds its echo in the radical evil occurring on the stage of history. They reflect each other as in the mirror. The melancholy of man, which is the deepest aspect of his being, finds its attunement in the profound melancholy of nature, as in a musical instrument where a touch in one string reverberates in all other strings. Writes Schelling:

> The most obscure and thus the deepest aspect of human nature is that of nostalgia [*Sehnsucht*], which is the inner gravity of the temperament, so to speak; in its most profound manifestation it appears as melancholy [*Schwermuth*]. It is by means of the latter that man feels a sympathetic relation to nature. What is most profound in nature is also melancholy; for it, too, mourns lost good, and likewise such an indestructible melancholy inheres in all forms of life because all life is founded upon something independent from itself (Schelling 1994, p. 230).

The metaphysics of life that Schelling constructs here is founded upon the principle of separation or cision. The separation of principles, the cision of existence from essence that is its ground, the relative independence of non-being (as Being in relation to itself) from being (*das Seyende*) and also, most importantly, the relative independence of man from God and nature: such separation is the very condition of possibility of all life, not only of the finite life of man and nature but even the divine life as well. It is on the basis of separation that revelation occurs on the stage of history, opening thereby the entire spiritual realm of the historical to a future redemption *to come* which is the eschatological possibility not only for man but for the entire finite world of existence.

Schelling has often been alleged of his anthropomorphic idea of God. However, a deeper understanding of the Schellingian notion of man discloses the paradoxical character of the place of man in the jointure of being. The privileged place of man, privileged insofar as he alone is the passage through which redemption passes through, is at once a non-place, the place of danger arising out of his demonic freedom, an empty measure where alone must take place the measureless measure of *eschaton*. As the in-between link between the divine life and nature, man is at the same the one in whom extremities touch: extremity of an immemorial past and future redemption coming from the other extremity of time, God on one hand and nature on the other, the melancholy of nature and the absolute beatitude in God. The place of man, this in-between, is thus a non-place, an *Atopos* yawned opened by the abyss of separation on the basis of which at all can there be communication among beings. Yet, this non-place that sets man apart from God and nature alike, while calling each towards him, is the very *taking place* of death as well as life, of disease as well as blissfulness, of poison as well as redemption, of violence as well as redemption to come. Schelling's eschatological drama of redemption thus presupposes a being whose privilege consists of its being bereft of all autochthony and sovereignty. It appears as if only as being non-sovereign, non-autochthonous and non-autarchic being, man can take his privileged part in this eschatological drama of redemption. *This non-sovereignty is the most fundamental principle of the Schellingian political eschatology.*

Already in 1809 essay on human freedom, Schelling understands this non-place where *the taking place* of revelation occurs as the groundless freedom of man. This borrowed freedom is gifted by God. Martin Heidegger rightly perceives here the most important contribution of Schelling to philosophy. Existence here is grasped as event (*Ereignis*), unthought and unthinkable in the traditional metaphysics of the West. From the predicative-judgmental-categorical structure of Occidental ontology, Schelling releases the eventive character of a finite existence. A non-sovereign and finite being (finite because of his non-sovereignty), he is yet open to the coming of redemption from an extremity of time; a historical existence but whose historicity consists of it being eschatological breaking open to the divine and nature alike. If *eschaton* is the fundamental principle of religion, then the sense of religion must be none other than the breaking open of all mythic immanence of autochthony and autarchy. This instance, far from being the concluding moment of the progressive historical becoming of the Occidental metaphysics, as Hegel saw his own moment to be, is rather like an instantaneous apparition of a lightning flash against an abyss of darkness. At this moment metaphysics takes a turn (*Kehre*). It is as if metaphysics itself turns against itself, bringing a most unthinkable caesura into its innermost ground of philosophy. With Schelling, philosophy becomes for the first time caesural, finite and non-sovereign thinking.

V. Metaphysics and Politics

The political stakes of Schelling's eschatology must be derived from his metaphysics of separation and we see Schelling himself drawing such stakes in the concluding part of his Stuttgart lecture of 1810. This is as follows—

Because of the fault of man—man who is the link, the hinge and the point of jointure—the continuity among beings are disjointed. Nature has lost its unity and its place in the continuity of beings in the same measure that man too has lost his natural unity with God and nature. Since man is granted a freedom on which basis he can create a new unity, man now creates a second natural unity "superimposed on the first" (Ibid., 227). It is a paradoxical unity in that it is both "artificial" (being the second nature) and "natural", insofar as it is "subject to the fate of all organic life, namely to bloom, to ripen, eventually to age, and finally to die" (Ibid.); "spiritual" (since it is created out of human freedom) and yet "material" (since it shares with materiality its imperfection). This artificial-natural and spiritual-material unity, this poor supplement of the lost unity and this violent imposition of this second nature is none other than the modern state.

"The natural unity", writes Schelling, "this second nature, superimposed on the first, to which man must necessarily take recourse, is the *state*; and to put it bluntly, the state is thus a consequence of the curse that has been placed on humanity. Because man no longer has God for his unity, he must submit to a material unity" (Ibid.).

The state thus, according to Schelling, bears the mark of the degradation and the fragility of man rather than the plenitude of his natural "goodness". Like the fallen man, the modern state is too, in the innermost constitution of its existence, is precarious and merely provisional. The modern state then belongs to the order of transiency, bereft of sovereignty and of the unconditional legitimacy of its being. Hence is the constant necessity felt by the state to legitimize its *raison d'être* by invoking a "moral setting"[31] that it lacks and by evoking the instance of exception, now becoming the norm of the state, in order to elicit absolute obligation from citizens. The state of exception, whether in the name of morality or in the name of a constant waging of war, becomes the *raison d'état*. The state acts like the principle of non-being which, due to its eternal lack of being, must constantly feel the malicious hunger to attain being (*das Seyende*). If, according to Schelling, the latter is the very condition of actualization of the radical evil and not a mere potentiality, then we can say that the radical evil is not a mere accidental result of the existence of the state but somehow belongs to its very constitution. The violence of the state and the violence of the order of the world-historical politics at large have to do with this aporetic foundation of the state. This aporia of the state is the very aporia of radical evil. Like the principle of non-being whose insatiable hunger for attainment of being intensifies more and more it falls below being (this is why it is *radically* evil) so that the devouring power of its actuality increases more and more and becomes empty of being, in a similar manner the instance of exception works and un-works for the state. In fact, Schelling says this without saying in such an explicit manner: at work (which is the very principle of its un-working) in the modern state is the principle of non-being itself which now and then turns into the worst form of despotism, even though this devouring power of non-being is attempted to be domesticated in order to reconcile the modern state with the existence of free beings. Schelling takes up three such discourses from his own time— namely, the French Revolution, Kantian concepts and Fichte's "closed Trade system"—which have attempted to "demonstrate how unity could possibly be reconciled with the existence of free beings; that is, the possibility of the state would, properly speaking, be but the condition for the highest possible freedom of the individuals" (Ibid.) and argues that all such attempts, destined to fail, can only turn out to be merely apologetic of the existing order of the world-historical politics. "Hence it is quite natural", deduces Schelling, "that the end of this period during which people have been talking of nothing but freedom, the most consequent minds, in their pursuit of the idea of a perfect state, would have arrived at the worst kind of despotism" (Ibid.).

The insufficiency and the precarious character of the state, instituted by the impoverished and insufficient action of the fallen man in order to supplement a lost unity, demands a second attempt to re-establish the lost unity similar to the original one, but this time by God himself. This is "revelation" that occurs in several stages till God himself must appear on the stage of history as man. Christ here is the mediator between God and man, in the way that man himself was the mediating link between God and nature before the link was broken by his fault. Now Christ is the passage from nature to God and his ignoble dying on the Cross is the abyss of suffering that must pass through nature to God so as to redeem all that is created.

Now the Church is the immediate consequence of the second revelation. Schelling's account of the origin of both the Church and the state here is deduced from his metaphysical framework of separation where the separation is conceived as an absolute event of *breaking away* or fall. If the event of breaking away or falling away (*Abfall*) would not have been there in the very jointure of beings as potentiality, then neither the state nor the Church would ever have come into being. Then the possibility and actuality of evil could only have been a mere privation of the good, a mere attenuated decrement emanating from the light of the good. Schelling draws here immense political consequences from such metaphysics of emanation. By denying the potentiality and actuality of the radical evil and by minimizing its terror into a necessary privation of the good to come in the process of a speculative-historical becoming, such theodicy of history would end up by justifying the violence of the order of the world-historical politics in the name of a future which it will never arrive. Or, such theodicy of history may end up glorifying the historical existence of an institution like the modern state as one of the figures of the absolute spirit that progressively masters the powers of the irrational into the institutional ground of Reason. The violence of the historical reason would then be justified. A century later, Benjamin transforms this Schellingian critique of historical Reason into a messianic deconstruction of "homogeneous empty time": how the past suffering of the vanquished and the oppressed is justified in the name of a quantitative, progressive approximation to a fulfilment deferred to a future that will never come.

The politico-theological import of the Schellingian eschatology must be measured against such a legitimizing theodicy of an empty historical process. In its ever vigilant critique of historical Reason, the Schellingian theological eschatology anticipates both the Marxist atheistic eschatological critique of the state and the church (followed by Ernst Bloch) and Kierkegaardian existential eschatological critique of historical Reason (followed and transformed by Franz Rosenzweig into a messianic deconstruction of the same). The Church is not immune from the Schellingian eschatological attack insofar as the Church, instead of remaining opposed to the powers of the world which it should be, according to its spirit, enters into alliance with the world-conquering powers of earthly sovereignties. Instead of remaining withdrawn from the external, violent unity instituted by the world-historical sovereignties, the Church now becomes the very theological foundation of the world-historical conquest. The result is a "one-dimensional humanity". The healthy separation of unities, principles and domains—external unity from internal one, non-being as the mere foundation of being (*das Seyende*), theological from the political—is collapsed into this most unspeakable terror of universal domination and "political tyranny".

> In surveying more recent history, which with good reason, is said to begin with the arrival of Christianity in Europe, we note that humanity had to pass through two stages in its attempt to discover or produce a unity; first that of producing an internal unity through the Church, which had to fail because the Church simultaneously sought to become the external unity and eventually attempted to produce external unity by means of the state. Only with the demise of hierarchical [systems] has the state attained this importance, and it is manifest that the pressure of political tyranny has increased ever since its exact proportion to be belief that an inner unity seemed dispensable; indeed it is bound to increase to a maximum intensity until, perhaps, upon the collapse of these one-dimensional attempts humanity will discover the right way" (Ibid., p. 229).

With the assumption of the external unity, the Church acts exactly like the modern state and in this manner they can collaborate in the triumphal project of the world-historical conquest. If that is so, then the sense of religion must not be exhausted in the axiomatic that is given by these world-historical institutions like the Church and the state. If *eschaton* is the fundamental sense of religion, and if *eschaton* implies separation, then this separation must inscribe itself, not so much between the Church and the state, but between religion and the political. Only then the one-dimensional attempts of humanity can be overcome.

Schelling conceives the name of "philosophical religion" as this overcoming of the one-dimensional humanity. Both the Church and the state are one-dimensional attempts, the first because it forgot the very spirit and promise of its existence and thus comes to be allied with the state, and the second because the state by its very existence as legitimizing institution, cannot but be one-dimensional. The radical evil is too one-dimensional, for it displaces the nexus of the two-fold powers and in a one-sided manner totalizes everything under the power of its non-being. Religion, on the other hand, is an overcoming of all such one-dimensional attempts in the name of true unity that is an eschatological potentiality. But this religion can only be understood as the religion to come, a future possibility, bound up with the messianic-apocalyptic redemption of mankind. This philosophical-religious concept of true unity or universality has an intrinsic relation to the advent, to the event of arrival, to the coming future in an essential sense, not the future that grows, ripens and passes away like the state, but the future always *to come*, a future for everyone and each one. This philosophical reason is truly universal, the universality implied in the very idea of philosophy and redemption. Schelling's idea of philosophical religion, always *to* come, is thus not the religion that already exists in being allied with the world-historical powers, but a *promised religion*, the religion of promise and hope. Here is Schelling again,

> Whatever the ultimate goal may turn out to be, this much is certain, namely, that true unity can be attained only *via* the path of religion; only the supreme and most diverse culture of religious knowledge will enable humanity, if not to abolish the state outright, then at least to ensure that the state will progressively divest itself of the blind force that governs it, and to transfigure this force into intelligence. It is not that the Church ought to dominate the state or vice-versa, but that the state ought to cultivate the religious principles within itself and that the community of all peoples ought to be founded on religious convictions that, themselves, out to become universal (Ibid., 229).

This is his eschatological hope. But this hope demands dissatisfaction with all possible one-dimensional attempts that human history till now bears witness. Schelling hereby anticipates the Kierkegaardian Christian eschatological critique of Christianity by separating religion from the political in such a way that religion itself cannot be completely conflated with the Church. This is to the extent that the Church itself has given up its true, inner unity for the sake of the external unity. Religion thereby must keep itself withdrawn from all the world-historical triumphalism.

To understand the immense ethico-political stakes of Schelling's political eschatology, it is not enough to understand him solely against the socio-historical-philosophical background of the early 19th

century. It is true that such consequences cannot be separated from Schelling's timely confrontations with the spirit of that age: his confrontation with and against the secularizing tendency of Enlightenment which gave rise to the modern state, his encounter with the totalizing theodicy of historical Reason that found such overpowering expression in the Hegelian grand system, and his tireless polemics with possible religious fanaticism implicit in thinkers like Jacobi, etc. It is also true that Schelling's timely eschatological double critique against the state and the Church alike prepared the way for Marx's atheistic eschatological critique of religion and the state and Kierkegaard's existential-theological critique of Christianity and the state. It is, however, a more interesting task to renew such an infinite critique of historical Reason when this historical Reason has assumed a more sophisticated and complex totalization in the form of neo-liberal "democratic" societies of today's world-historical order. If such a renewal of the critique of historical Reason is an inescapable task today, then Schellingian political eschatology with its insistence on messianic-eschatological promise and hope seems indispensable for us. At the beginning of the last century, we see transformation of Schelling's Christian eschatology into the atheistic messianism of revolution of Ernst Bloch and into the liturgical-existential messianism of Franz Rosenzweig. It is interesting to observe that Schelling can appeal to Marx and Kierkegaard alike as much as he attracts both Bloch and Rosenzweig. In that sense, the historical-contemporary understanding of Schelling in his own time, that Schelling is merely a conservative windbag, was mistaken. This shows how misplaced and limited a historical understanding can be. The renewal of Schellingian thinking today, whether one assumes one side (atheistic eschatology/messianism) or the other (theological eschatology/messianism), must learn from this history of reception of Schellingian thought one important lesson: that the task of philosophy and religion, or more appropriately, "philosophical religion" in the Schellingian sense, is to conceive of a deconstructive strategy of delegitimation of sovereignty of all worldly powers, whether the state or the Church, in such a manner that, through an intensification of difference, the promise of a future must be kept open, a future always *to come*. It is Schelling coming before Marx and Nietzsche, more than anyone of the early 19th century, who attempted to philosophize out of the messianic-eschatological future, a philosophical task that is still ours.

NOTES

1. It is in his *Bruno* which is written as a dialogue, modelled upon Platonic dialogues, wherein Schelling presents the Platonic notion of constellation (Schelling 1984).
2. This shows how Hegel's remark on Schelling in the Preface to his *Phenomenology of Spirit*—a remark that dealt a death blow to Schelling's philosophy—is unjustified. We read in Hegel: "To pit this single insight, that in the Absolute everything is the same, against the full body of articulated cognition which at least seeks and demands such fulfilment, to palm off its Absolute as the night in which, as the saying goes, all cows are black—this is cognition naively reduced to vacuity" (Hegel 1998, p. 9).
3. In this sense, it is only Walter Benjamin's Platonism that approaches the Schellingian Platonism of ideas as essences. Like Schelling, Benjamin in the "Epistemo-Critical Prologue" of his *Origin of German Tragic Drama* conceives the relation of truth and beauty in the Platonic manner: ideas are essences entering in a constellation wherein their singularity is preserved, without subsuming them into the concept: "Ideas are timeless constellations, and by virtue of the elements being seen as points in such constellations, phenomena are subdivided and at the same time redeemed..." (Benjamin 1998, p. 34). Benjamin thus takes the task of philosophy to be "the salvation of phenomena and the representation of ideas" (Ibid., p. 35).
4. Again here one can see the proximity of Benjamin with Schelling. Like Schelling who understands potencies as stars wherein each such celestial body, in its own singular manner, reflects the entire universal and where each potency is, in its very finitude, a reflection of the infinite; so Benjamin conceives every idea as a sun, "related other ideas just as suns are related to each other. The harmonious relationship between such essences is what constitutes truth"(Ibid., p. 37). Apart from the influence of Plato on both Schelling and Benjamin, it is Leibniz's idea of monadology wherein the idea of truth is conceived musically, that is,

as "harmony" that is decisively important for both these thinkers. For a careful discussion of the importance of Leibniz for Benjamin in this respect, I refer to the fourth chapter "Melancholy and Truth" of Ilit Ferber's book *Philosophy and Melancholy: Benjamin's Early Reflections on Theatre and Language* (2013).

5. For Schelling, eschatological arrival of eternity, truly conceived, is not to be understood as mere endlessness of time, time that is prolonged to an endless duration, a homogeneous endless empty infinite. Schelling rather conceives—like Benjamin later—eternity of beatitude as "timeless" and thus "ahistorical": "the soul is not eternal because its duration is without beginning or end but rather because it has no relationship to time at all. Therefore it cannot be called immortal in a sense that would include an individual continuity. Since this could not be conceived of independent of finitude and the body, immortality would only be continued mortality and an ongoing imprisonment of the soul rather than a liberation" (Schelling 2010, p. 47). Between eternity and time, immortality and finitude there is a discontinuity, a caesura and a rupture that cannot be bridged by a continuous movement of a homogeneous time endlessly extended to the infinite. Later both Benjamin and Rosenzweig in his *The Star of Redemption,* each in his own way, understand the idea of discontinuity and interruption in a messianic manner. Schelling's eschatology is thus founded upon the idea of discontinuity and interruption between what exists as finite and what is to come from an extremity of the future.
6. While in schematic mode of representation the particular is intuited through the universal, in allegorical mode of representation the universal is intuited through the particular. The synthesis of schematic and allegorical is the symbolic mode of representation. In a strict sense, according to Schelling, mythology can be understood only symbolically and in that sense only Greek art is symbolic: "Mythology as such and every poetic rendering of it in particular are to be comprehended neither schematically nor allegorically, but rather symbolically" (Schelling 1989, p. 48).
7. Archetypes or ideas—which are the contents of mythology—are the individuated absolute. Schelling also calls them potencies. Schelling deduces the idea of mythology in the following manner: "The absolute is absolutely one; viewed absolutely in particular forms, however, such that the absolute is thereby not suspended this one =idea. The same holds true for art. It, too, views or intuits primal beauty only in ideas as particular forms, each of which, however, is divine and absolute for

itself. Whereas philosophy intuits these ideas as they are in *themselves*, art intuits them *objectively*. The universal symbolism or universal *representation* of the *ideas* as real is thus given in mythology..."(Ibid., p. 17).

8. Schelling writes, "All of ancient history can be viewed as the tragic period of history. Fate, too, is a form of providence, except that it is intuited within the real, just as providence is fate intuited in the ideal. Eternal necessity reveals itself during the time of identity with it as nature. This was the case with the Greeks. After the fall from nature it reveals itself in bitter and violent blows as fate. One can escape fate only in one way: by throwing oneself into the arms of providence...The old gods lost their power, the oracles and celebrations fell silent, and a bottomless abyss full of a wild admixture of all the elements of the past world appeared to open itself up before mankind. Above this dark abyss the only sign of peace and of a balance of forces seems to the cross, a kind of rainbow of a second flood..." (Ibid., p. 61).
9. Thus the notion of "caesura" or "separation" (*Scheidung*) of Schellingian philosophical eschatology assumes here a political-theological intonation. In fact, this is precisely the aim of my essay here: to show that the Schellingian eschatology of caesura may be understood as his political-theological conception par excellence, not that Schelling explicitly formulated such a political theology anywhere but rather that it is to be found as the spirit of his thought as such. For discussions on Gnosticism in its fundamental conception of "worldlessness", I refer to Hans Jonas' justly famous *The Gnostic Religion* (2001) and Adolf Harnack's *Marcion: The Gospel of the Alien God* (2007). Jacob Taubes in his various essays published together as *From Cult to Culture* (2010) and in his doctorate dissertation *Occidental Eschatology* (2009), draws profound political-theological implications of the concept of caesura or setting apart. Thus one reads in the very concluding paragraph of Taubes' astonishing dissertation (in its published version): "The measure of God is holy. First of all the holy is separation and setting apart. The holy is the terror that shakes the foundations of the world. The shock caused by the holy, bursts asunder the foundations of the world for salvation. It is the holy that passes judgment in the court of history. History exists only when truth is separated from error, when truth is illuminated from mystery. History is elucidated from the mystery of error to the revelation of truth" (2009, p. 194). Tracing a genealogy of the eschatological thoughts of 19th century Europe and even the contemporary thought of Taubes' own time back to early Jewish

apocalypticism, the Prophetic tradition of the Bible and Gnosticism in various forms, Taubes argues here that at stake of Occidental eschatology lies the vision, suppressed by the triumphant march of world-historical politics, the vision of liberation of the oppressed and vanquished from the cages of the world. The liberation thus presupposes the separation of the world *to come* from the foundation of the world as it exists under the various regimes of earthly sovereignty. The notion of the holy —as setting apart—is this eschatological principle par excellence, which is also the very setting apart of the religious, which in its true impulse is eschatological, from its admixture with the political impulse of legitimizing the worldly sovereignties as they exist allied with the order of the universal world-history.

10. Thus Schelling writes of Christ: "The incarnate God is not an enduring, eternal figure, but rather only a manifestation preordained from eternity but transitory in time. In Christ, it is rather the finite that is symbolized by the infinite than the latter by the former. Christ returns to the super sensible world but promises not himself but rather the spirit, and not the principle that will enter into and abide in the finite but the ideal principle that is to lead all of the finite into and to the infinite...the true god has to become finite in order to demonstrate in himself the nullification of the finite. To the extent Christ was simultaneously the apex and the end of the world of the gods of antiquity. This proves that the appearance of Christ, far from being the beginning of a new polytheism, was rather the absolute conclusion of this world of the gods" (Ibid., p. 64).
11. For a fascinating discussion of St. Paul's eschatology and messianism in relation to Jewish Gnosticism, I refer to Jacob Taubes' lecture on St. Paul, published posthumously as *The Political Theology of Paul* (2003).
12. In his Schelling inspired *Atheism in Christianity*, Ernst Bloch makes the idea of exodus fundamental not only to Christianity and Jewish religion but to religion as such and understands this idea of exodus as a radical atheism which adheres in religion as such and in Christianity in particular. Founded upon his idea of the Ontology of Not Yet, Bloch understands the religion of exodus to be opening for us the most radical possibility where the world-dominating earthly powers undergo the nullity of their legitimacy, rendering the realm of history an open ending eschatological process. Bloch thus perceives the historical world as it is exists now as still indeterminate, pregnant with unforeseeable potentiality not yet actualized; the home not reached and the unconditional fulfilment, which alone can be redemptive, not yet

attained on earth. The spirit and the promise of Christianity for Bloch, far from being a religion of vain consolation in a beyond, is this exodus passion where hope for the unconditional is born anew every day, a passion which Bloch calls "atheism" (see Bloch 1972). Jürgen Moltmann, following Bloch in this respect, transforms Bloch's atheistic eschatological principle of hope into the theological principle of Christian eschatology par excellence (see Moltmann 2004 & 1993).

13. In the first chapter "The Nameless Good" of his book *Conspiracy of Life: Meditations on Schelling and His Time,* Jason Wirth convincingly argues that for Schelling the question of the ethical is of prime importance (see Wirth 2003, pp. 5-32).
14. Schelling offers here three forms of reflective cognition: categorical, hypothetical and disjunctive (Ibid., pp. 12-5).
15. "All philosophizing begins, writes Schelling, "with the idea of the Absolute come alive. That which is true can only be recognized in truth; that which is evident, in evidence" (Schelling 2010, p. 15).
16. "This view", writes Schelling, "which is as evident as it is noble, also represents the true Platonic doctrine put forward in the aforementioned writings and carries most purely and distinctively the imprint of its founder's spirit. According to Plato, the soul can descend from its original state of beatitude and be borne into the temporal universe and thereby torn away from the truth only by means of a falling away from the originary image. This was the tenet of the Greek mystery cult's secret teachings, to which Plato alluded quite explicitly : that the origin of the phenomenal world should not be imagined, as popular religion does, as *creation*, as positive emersion from the Absolute but as a falling away from it. Hereupon was founded its practical doctrine that the soul, the fallen divine essence in man, must be withdrawn from and purified of its relation and association with the flesh as much as possible so that by mortifying the sensate life the soul can regain absoluteness and again partake of the intuition of the originary image" (Ibid., p. 27).
17. Schelling here distinguishes his concept of non-being from nothingness.
18. Similarly Schelling writes in Bruno: "In the heavenly bodies, the elements whereby things separate themselves and distance themselves from the image of identity is not divorced from the element whereby they are assimilated into the infinite concept, and they are not split up into contending forces. Instead their elements are harmoniously yoked, and just as they alone are truly immortal, so these heavenly beings alone enjoy the blessed condition of reality as a whole, even in the state

of separated existence ...you should therefore think of the planets' course of motion as something perfectly whole and simple, not a composite of forces, but an absolute identity thereof. One of the factors of this identity [centripetal force] causes a thing to inhere within the identity of all things; it is commonly called gravity. The other is [centrifugal force] which causes a thing to reside in itself; we commonly view it as opposite of gravity. But these are absolutely equivalent forms of the identity that constitutes the planet's motion; both are the same totality, one thing in fact " (Schelling 1984, p. 169).

19. Schelling compares the whole eschatology of history as an epic with two parts: "History is an epic composed in the mind of God. It has two main parts: one depicting mankind's egress from its centre to its furthest point of displacement; the other, its return. The former is, as it were, history's Iliad; the latter, it's Odyssey. In the one, the direction is centrifugal; in the latter it becomes centripetal. In this way, the grand purpose of the phenomenal world reveals itself in history. The ideas, the spirits, must fall away from the centre and insert themselves into the particularity of nature, the general realm of the falling away, so that afterwards, and as particularities, they may return to indifference and, reconciled with it, may be able to abide in it without disturbing it" (Ibid., pp. 44-45).
20. Of non-being as the foundation of being (*das Seyende*) of God, Schelling writes : " This is indeed a non-being in that it originally relates to Him merely as the foundation, as that which He Himself is not, or as that which exists merely as the basis for that which truly is. And yet it is also a being in and of itself " (Schelling 1994, p. 209).
21. See "The Doctrine of Being" of Hegel's *Logic* (1975).
22. In this Schellingian idea of contraction of God has its unmistakable resonance in the Lurianic school of Kabbalah. As Gershom Scholem writes of this resonance : "The following quotation from the German philosopher reads like a description of the *Tsimtsum* and its significance for the personality of God: "Alles Bewusstsein ist Konzentration, ist Samlung, ist Zusammennehmen, seiner selbst. Diese vereinende, auf es selbst, zuruckgehende Kraft eines Wesens ist die wahre Kraft der Personalichkeit in ihm, die Kraft der selbheit" (see Scholem 1995, p. 412).
23. This act of contraction in God can only be understood as the decision of God arising out of his absolute freedom. Thus Schelling writes: "This act of restriction or descent on the part of God is spontaneous. Hence the explanation of the world has no other ground than the freedom of

God. Only God Himself can break with the absolute identity of His essence and thereby can create the space for a revelation" (Schelling 1994, p. 204).

24. Of this primordial separation, Schelling writes: "Hence, once God has separated Himself internally, He has separated Himself *qua* being from his Being...whoever does not separate himself from his Being considers this *Being* essential rather than his inner superior, and more truthful essence. Likewise, if God were to remain as immersed in his Being, there would be no life, no growth. Hence, He separates Himself from his being precisely because it is merely a tool for Him" (Ibid., p. 209).
25. Schelling conceives this simultaneity of difference in the following manner: "God posits Himself as the first power, as something unconscious; however, he cannot concentrate His self into the Real without expanding as the Ideal, that is, He cannot posit Himself as the Real, as an object, without positing Himself *simultaneously* as a subject; and both of these constitute *one Act* of absolute simultaneity; with His actual concentration into the Real, God also posits His expansion as the Ideal (Ibid., 207).
26. "[Non] being relates to God as the flower relates to the sun. Although the flower emanates from the dark earth only through the efficacy of the sun and is transformed by light, there nevertheless remains always something whose very root exists independently of this [flower]. If the relation of man to God was not of this kind he would not have any freedom with respect to God and would be but a ray of sunlight or a spark of fire" (Ibid., 224).
27. In Deleuze's remarkable words: " The most important aspect of Schelling's philosophy is his consideration of powers. How unjust, in this respect, is Hegel's critical remark about the black cows! Of these two philosophers, it is Schelling who brings difference out of the night of the Identical, and with finer, more varied and more terrifying flashes of lightning than those of contradiction: with *progressivity*. Anger and love are powers of the Idea which develop on the basis of a *më* on—in other words, not from a negative or a non-being [*ouk on*] but from a problematic being or non-existent, a being implicit in those existences beyond the ground. The God of love and the God of anger are required in order to have an idea. A, A2, A3 form the play of pure depotentialisation and potentiality, testifying to the presence in Schelling's philosophy of a differential calculus adequate to the dialectic" (Deleuze 1994, pp. 190-91).

28. Schelling understands this independence of man from both God and nature as the mark of his freedom. "Those who defend freedom", writes Schelling, "are ordinarily concerned with demonstrating man's independence from nature, which is indeed an easy matter. However, they fail to consider man's inner independence from God and his freedom, relative to God, which is most difficult to demonstrate" (Schelling 1994, p. 225).
29. In his lecture on Schelling's 1809 essay on freedom, Martin Heidegger discusses Schelling's notion of jointure (Heidegger 1985).
30. For a lovely discussion of this Schellingian concept, see Jason Wirth's introduction to *The Ages of the World* (Schelling 2000, pp. vii-xxxii)
31. Thus Schelling could say: "The state, even if it being governed in a rational manner, knows well that its material power alone cannot effect anything and that it must invoke higher and spiritual motives. These, however, lie beyond its domain and cannot be controlled by the state, even though the latter boasts with being able to create a moral setting, thereby arrogating to itself a power equal to nature. A free spirit, however, will never consider such a natural unity sufficient, and a higher talisman is required; consequently, any unity that originates in the state remains inevitably precarious and provisional" (Ibid.).

REFERENCES

Benjamin, Walter, *The Origin of the German Tragic Drama*, trans. John Osborne (New York: Verso, 1998).

Bloch, Ernst, *Atheism in Christianity*, trans. Peter Thompson (New York: Verso, 1972).

Deleuze, Gilles, *Difference and Repetition*, trans. Paul Patton (London: The Athlone Press, 1994).

Ferber, Ilit, *Melancholy and Philosophy: Benjamin's Early Reflections on Theatre and Language* (Stanford & California: Stanford University Press, 2013).

Harnack, Adolf, *Marcion: The Gospel of the Alien God* (Engene, regon: Wipf & Stock Publishers, 2007).

Hegel, G.W.F., *Phenomenology of Spirit*, trans. A.V. Miller (Delhi: Motilal Benarasidass, 1998).

Hegel, G.W.F., *Logic*, trans. William Wallace with a Foreword by J. N. Findley (Oxford: Clarendon Press, 1975).

Heidegger, Martin, *Schelling's Treatise on the Essence of Human Freedom,* trans. Stambaugh, J. (Athens: Ohio University Press, 1985).

Jonas, Hans, *The Gnostic Religion* (Boston: Beacon Press, 2001).

Moltmann, Jürgen, *Theology of Hope: On the Ground and the Implications of a Christian Eschatology*, trans. James W. Leitch (Minneapolis: Fortress Press, 1993).

Moltmann, Jürgen. *The Coming of God: Christian Eschatology*, trans. Margaret Kohl (Minneapolis: Fortress Press, 2004).

Schelling, F.W.J von., *The Philosophy of Art*, trans. Douglas W. Stott (Minneapolis: University of Minnesota Press, 1989).

Schelling, F.W.J. von, *Philosophy and Religion*, trans. Klaus Ottmann (Putnam, Conn.: Spring Publications, 2010).

Schelling, F.W.J. von, *Bruno or On the Natural and the Divine Principle of Things*, trans. Michael G. Vater (Albany: State University of New York, 1984).

Schelling, F.W.J. von, "Stuttgart Seminars" in *Idealism and the Endgame of Theory*, trans. Thomas Pfau (Albany: State University of New York Press, 1994), pp. 195-243.

Scholem, Gershom, *Major Trends in Jewish Mysticism*, Foreword by Robert Alter (New York: Schocken Books, 1995).

Taubes, Jacob, *The Political Theology of Paul*, trans. Dana Hollander (Stanford: Stanford University Press, 2003).

Taubes, Jacob, *Occidental Eschatology*, trans. David Ratmoko (Stanford: Stanford University Press, 2009).

Jacob Taubes, *From Cult to Culture: Fragments Toward a Critique of Historical Reason,* ed. Charlotte Elisheva Fonrobert (Stanford: Stanford University Press, 2010).

Wirth, Jason, *The Conspiracy of Life: Meditations on Schelling and His Time* (Albany: State University of New York, 2003).

Wirth, Jason, "Translator's Introduction" to *The Ages of the World* (Albany: State University of New York Press, 2000).

5

Nationalism, Colonialism and Modern Linguistics

Franson Manjali

Introduction

In spite of the contemporary claims regarding a universal grammar, it is a well-known fact that languages of the world differ in indefinitely many ways, and similarly, the ways in which scholars have approached and studied languages are also irreducibly diverse. If linguistic theories and practices in ancient and medieval times, especially in the Hebraic, Indian Latin and Arab traditions, have had a religious orientation, what can be noticed in the modern contexts is a strong orientation in issues directly or indirectly political. When a language is not viewed as having its provenance in God, and when the humans have to decide and determine its use and its fate in the mundane milieu, then political issues are often called upon to respond to the questions of language.

Languages have not only been those in which God's word is supposed to be revealed to the humans, or the mode in which he or she submits to Him, but also those by which man orders the living world of people and things. Languages have stood not only by God, but have aided empires and nations. It is said that before the Spanish sailors sailed to conquer the New World, the scholar Anton de Nebrija recommended to Queen Isabel his then newly published grammar of Castilian (1492) with the observation that "language was always the companion of empire... language and empire began, increased, and flourished together" (Quoted in Errington, J. 2008, p. 18).

Besides employing languages for religious persuasion, humans have imposed their languages and their linguistic perspectives on their own communities and on other peoples whom they dominated. Between the assumed verbal power of an almighty God and the hapless day-to-day linguistic existence of ordinary humans, between nations and between human communities, there has always been the exercise of linguistic power as well as its resistance. When we notice it is these linguistic confrontations that make up much of the history of our world, it becomes amply clear, contrary to appearance, that political innocence has been more of an exception than a norm in the linguistic domain.

It is not difficult to see historically instances of how linguistic power operates either within the context of one's own community or nation, or across national boundaries where direct political domination exists. Bernard Cohn (1996) has succinctly described the exercise of British linguistic power in the early colonial Indian context:

> The years 1770 to 1785 may be looked upon as the formative period during which the British successfully began the programme of appropriating Indian languages to serve a crucial component in their construction of the system of rule. More and more British officials were learning the "classical" languages of India (Sanskrit, Persian, and Arabic) as well as many "vulgar" languages. More importantly, this was the period in which the British were beginning to produce an apparatus: grammars, dictionaries, treatises, class books, and translations about and from languages of India. ... (T)he production of these texts and others that followed them began the establishment of discursive formation, defined as epistemological space, created a discourse (Orientalism), and had the effect of converting Indian form of knowledge into European objects. The subjects of these texts were first and foremost the Indian languages themselves, represented in European terms as grammars, dictionaries, and teaching aids in a project to make the acquisition of a working knowledge of the language available to those British who were to be part of the ruling group in India (Cohn 1996, pp. 20-21).

1. The European Context

We shall begin by considering the early modern period in Europe, also referred to as the "classical" era. It is useful for us to see that political linguistics have manifested in multiple ways in the European context. Perhaps, we may mention as the *first* approach the path opened up by Benedict Anderson in his well-known work, *Imagined Communities* and see how languages became the basis of nationalism and nation-formation in Europe. The *second* is to follow the one proposed by Michel Foucault (1966), where the very discourses pertaining to language within what emerged as "the human sciences" underwent specific discontinuities, first from the Renaissance period to the Classical period, and then from the latter to the Modern period. As a *third* approach we shall try and follow how philosophical ideas, such as those of John Locke, Condillac and Johann G. Herder, emphasized the *voluntary* and *creative* use of language in individuals' expressions, in relation to both scientific and popular knowledge formations. Related to this is a *fourth* issue, also closely connected to what Edward Said had famously identified as the discourse of Orientalism, which is clearly evident in the works of William Jones, Wilhelm von Humboldt and Max Müller, among others.

We are here concerned with the question: how did the European colonizations affect the balance of power between languages and cultures in that continent? Philology began with the contact and the "command" the European scholars established with the cultural and linguistic brought into the continent. The comparative and historical studies that philologists undertook, had the effect of levelling out on the one hand of the Judeo-Christian languages and their associated worldviews (of Hebrew, Greek and Latin) and those of the newly discovered and attested languages. And on the other hand, it led to the preferential acceptance and treatment of certain languages or groups of languages over certain others. In the new global linguistic family and kinship system, certain languages and their corresponding "families", such as Sanskrit and other classical Indo-European languages were favoured and others, such as Chinese and Arabic were relegated to an inferior and under-developed status. The ideological biases of such scholarly positions, often springing from previously internalized philosophical and religious beliefs could only be prejudicial and therefore devoid of the intended scientific basis.[1]

2. Emergence of National Languages

Anderson (1983) focuses on the material substructure of the formation of European "national languages" which started appearing in the 14th century (English, 1382) and began to accelerate from the 16th century with the declaration of Français (1539) as the official language in his dominion by the French King François I, who in fact named the new language after himself.

Anderson has described how in the context of the emergence of capitalism and print-technology, European vernaculars were assembled into "print-languages" and how the latter with the aid of "print-capitalism" became the basis for the emergence of national consciousness, and eventually the nation states. This process, he notes, further entailed:

(a) the creation of "unified fields of exchange and communication below Latin and above the vernaculars";
(b) providing "a new fixity to language, which ... helped to build the image of antiquity so central to the idea of the nation";
(c) the creation of new "'languages of power' of a kind different from the older administrative vernaculars." (1991: 44-45)

Anderson emphasizes that "the fixing of print-languages and the differentiation of status between them were *largely unself-conscious* processes resulting from the explosive interaction between capitalism, technology and the human linguistic diversity." (p. 45) (italics mine)

3. The Discourse of Language

Foucault observes a somewhat parallel movement involving a discontinuity from a discourse of "resemblance" during the Renaissance period to that of "representation" in the Classical period. In the latter period, things in nature do not signify by means of words that were thought to naturally resemble them, but it is now the rationally endowed man who "represents" by means of signs the ideas that correspond to things. The authors of the Cartesian-inspired Port-Royal grammar (1660) wrote that signs are not naturally present, but are "invented" by man.

The historical period that Anderson considered in which national languages begin to take shape is that of early European modernity, which somewhat coincided with what Foucault calls the "classical" period of the 17th century, that is, the period preceding that of "Enlightenment", or the "modern" period that begins in the late 18th century. Foucault, in his *The Order of Things* (1966), discusses the latter period that harbingered the "comparison" of languages and study of their historical changes. This was the beginning of comparative philology, which in many ways paved the way for modern linguistics of the 19th and 20th centuries.

Foucauldian "archaeology" sees this emergence of comparatism and historicism as the second major "discontinuity" in European linguistic thought (along with other similar discontinuities in economics and biology). This discontinuity from the classical to the modern period is characterized by a shift from understanding language as "representation" by means of *signs*, to the study of the historical changes in the *form* of languages by way of comparison. As Foucault states it:

> In the last quarter of the 18th century, the horizontal comparison of languages... no longer makes it possible to know what each language may still preserve of its ancestral memory, what marks from before Babel have been preserved in the sounds of its words, but it should make it possible to measure the extent to which languages resemble one another, the density of their similitudes, the limits within which they are transparent to one another (Foucault 1966/1970, p. 233).

Such comparisons between languages, Foucault says, involved "great confrontations between various languages", which sometimes reflected "pressures of political motive".[2]

In these "confrontations" between languages, Foucault rightly identifies the emergence of the grammatical "inflection" as the "form intermediary between articulation of contents and the value of roots."

(Ibid., p. 234) We note here that the grammatical property of "inflection" became the basis of the comparison between and the so-called classical languages, Sanskrit, Greek and Latin, by Gaston Cœurdoux and Sir William Jones, and particularly the basis of the latter's claim regarding the superiority (and for some, the near-perfection) of Sanskrit even among these "classical" languages. Foucault is silent about the ideological elevation of these classical "Indo-European" (and for some, "Aryan") languages, but he rightly notes the decisive role played by "inflection" in the birth of modern linguistics.[3] By the end of the 18th century, he says:

> ... through the inflectional system, the dimension of the purely grammatical is appearing: language no longer consists of representations and of sounds that in turn represent the representations and are ordered among them as the links of thought require; it consists also of formal elements, grouped into a system, which impose upon the sounds, syllable and roots an organization that is not that of representation. Thus an element has been introduced into the analysis of language that is not reducible to it. (Ibid., p. 235)

Right as he is to the emergence of philology as a modern historical science, Foucault's "archaeology" is decidedly averse to seeing the *ideological* dimensions that accompanied this discontinuity. Edward Said (still inadequately) and others have focused on the central role that philology played in the formation of the bourgeoning field of "Orientalism". Said quotes Benjamin Disraeli at the start of his book: "The East is a career." (Said, 1979, xii) It could be added that the "Orient" was a prestigious and productive career for the European bourgeoisie in the late 18th and 19th centuries that aided the colonial expansions in providing the cultural and political directions. In other words, they were evidently motivated by political and religious ideologies in the wake of the economic gains that colonialism had begun to accrue.

4. Rationalism and Empiricism in Language Studies

Grammatical studies of the "classical" 17th century were characterized, in a properly Cartesian manner, by the emergence of the notion of "innate ideas" and the mental operations with them as what words stand for or represent. As per the classic opening definition of the General and Rational Grammar of Port-Royal:

> Grammar is the art of speaking. Speaking is explaining one's thoughts by signs which men have invented for this purpose....

In this formulation, signs are the means by which one expresses innately present ideas and explain to others one's logically organized thoughts. Knowledge, according to Cartesian rationalism, does not naturally emerge from the world, but is produced by human beings on the basis of their innate ideas and mental operations involving them. Signs, for their part, involve a material part, the sounds or letters and the ideal part, "signification", which is the specific manner in which one uses the former to "signify" one's thoughts generated by the universal rational apparatus. Grammar is no more concerned with the "signs of things" as it was the case for the medieval "modistae" grammarians (e.g. Thomas of Erfurt). It is no more the natural "things" that the natural signs signify. Signs invented by man now signify innate and rational ideas.

This picture of the interrelationship between the innately endowed knowledge and the "invented" signs of language was substantially transformed and altered by John Locke in the late 17th century. Rejecting Cartesian Rationalism, Locke claimed that the signs that constitute language do not pre-exist the corresponding ideas. Just as he maintained in his empiricist theory that ideas arise by transforming the sensations received from the external world, he would insist that words are obtained by voluntarily imposing upon articulate sounds marks in order to remember and recognize particular ideas. Since the imposition of a mark is voluntary and devoid of any prior necessity, a sign can bear only an *arbitrary* relationship with the corresponding idea.

Thus, according to Locke, linguistic signs come to exist only by way of voluntary acts of human individuals. They do not exist as a random set for man to choose from in their communicative needs, but rather they have to be wilfully created in specific experiential situations. There is no common, universal human invention of the sign. Signs are the result of voluntary impositions of many different individuals, and that is what in Locke's view, renders them prone to error or "imperfections".

According to Locke, ideas may be formed from the things in a more or less correct or perfect manner, but what words do primarily is to "signify" or "stand for" the ideas, by means of the voluntary and imposed marks which as signs help humans in recording their own thoughts, to assist them in fixing their own memory, and to present and to transfer their ideas to others. Locke suggests an extreme degree of individuality of linguistic signs. Words signify the particular ideas formed by individual speakers. One's idea about a particular thing expressed in one's own words cannot be the same idea of another that he would express by his words. There are no signs in general corresponding to things. He says:

> Words being voluntary Signs, they cannot be voluntary Signs imposed by him on Things that he knows not.

Locke can be seen to take his empiricism to an extreme, even if he is dealing with "ideas" at the level of language and knowledge. Sensations are received from things, and they are transformed into ideas. The individual imposes marks on the sounds or sound sequences corresponding to the ideas he has formed. This results in the arbitrariness of signs. The scenario is rather uncomplicated at the level of simple ideas of things and the corresponding signs, which tend to be somewhat similar for most individuals. However, the complex ideas (in the higher intellectual domains) got by compounding of simple ideas and the signs for them are never the same for all individuals. This disparity involving the signs and ideas for oneself, as well as that between the ideas of different individuals in conversation and argumentation in fact renders ordinary language more of a hindrance than an aid in communication. Locke refers to this as the "imperfection" of words in relation to ideas, and correcting these imperfections is one of his main philosophical goals. The imperfections are to be remedied by providing stable "definitions" of words and their meanings. And the definitions have to be arrived at particularly for the complex terms, by determining what kind of metaphorical extensions have been made from the simple ideas got on the basis of the initial sensations.

For Locke, the sphere of knowledge exists for man by way of individual expressions of ideas, and acts of language are the only mode in which they can be expressed. And since, people often connect their ideas with words that are imperfect, the corresponding knowledge too is likely to be erroneous. So the epistemological and linguistic investigations and processes can go in two different directions: *a.* by noting the original sensation-based ideas and the subsequent metaphorical extensions upon them a core vocabulary can be determined, and *b.* permitting the continuous historical expansion of the correctly formed words and thus obtaining correct knowledge on the basis of the former. From such a position, both knowledge (mind) and language are regarded as interdependent as well in constant and dynamic historical progression. The human mind does not evolve from mere internal logical operations involving ideas and already invented signs (as believed by the rationalists), but consists of acts that begin with receiving sensation(s) from the external world, individually and privately transforming the sensations into ideas, conveying one's own ideas to others by means of the voluntarily created words in a conduit process, philosophically determining the imperfections of words, remedying them on the basis of a metaphorical understanding of their etymology and thus permitting the historical progress of language and therefore of humanity.

5. Origin and Historical Development of Languages

Etienne Bonnot Abbé de Condillac, Locke's keen follower in France, was more directly and more intensely concerned with the question of language. He was speculating on the natural and historical origins of language and its development to higher and higher degrees of progress by means of analysis of language in relation to the thinking process. The better one undertakes this linguistic analysis, the better would be one's ability to think. Thinking, Condillac declares, is "the art of speaking."

Thus, Condillac's interest lies not just in the question of obtaining the right knowledge, but rather in how language enables thinking. Highest forms of *thinking*, *judging* and *reasoning*, are undertaken with words, and he claims, "just as we calculate with numerals, and languages are for ordinary people what algebra is for the geometricians" (Quoted in Harris and Taylor, 1997, pp. 137-38). For Condillac, man needs to have a voluntary control over the signs of language and their use not only to remember things but even more to reflect and to think. Higher forms of thinking can take place only with the acquisition and use of language. Language is the material substance upon which man has been able to build his edifice of thinking. And this is done by analysis of language in relation to the mind. We analyse the linear structure of language into its components and their organization, in order to understand the corresponding structure of thinking.

This approach is evident from Condillac's classification of signs into *accidental* signs, *natural* signs and *institutional* or *artificial* signs. Artificial signs of language, voluntarily created by man, have raised him from a state of nature, unlike the case with the beasts. It has provided him with the faculty of thinking. Condillac elaborates on how the analysis of language and therefore of thought is conducted on the basis of their parallelism with human gestures which he considers to be natural. Just as we mentally analyse the natural gestures involved in basic human communication, we analyse the corresponding language into its components. This analogical connection (which is common for all men) is the material basis of human communication, and it does away with the initial non-generative requirement of arbitrariness in the constitution and use of signs. Thus, on the basis of gestural analysis, and its continuous adoption in language, there is analogical creativity all the way in language from its very human inception. Thus, the signs begin with a natural connection with gestures, but are continuously and progressively humanized in history, by way of analogical creativity. Human mental analytical ability and his "will" take his language and thinking ever forward in history. Non-arbitrariness of linguistic signs and their combinations attained by way of analogical creation from the natural gestures aid in inter-human communication and understanding. And this analogical process may be consciously undertaken, even though it could be present even unconsciously.

However, though language and thinking involve a natural growth and development by men from a natural gestural base by way of analogical principles, Condillac insists that this process of linguistic and mental development is not uniform across different cultures, for the patterns and the quality of analogical creation are not the same in different contexts. Humans analogise in a better or worse manner to produce a superior or inferior mental and linguistic development in relation to nature's fount of knowledge which is available for all mankind. And since our thoughts are dependent on how well we analyse our language, the latter has a determining role in our knowledge development.

> Since our languages which take form in proportion as we analyse them, became so many analytical methods, it is understandable that we find it natural to think according to the habits that they cause us to acquire. We think with them. Rulers of our judgment, they determine our knowledge, opinions and prejudices. In short, they do in this domain everything good or bad... (Quoted in Ibid., p. 133).

Furthermore, our first naturally available and gesture-based language is the most appropriate rational language. Therefore it is best that a people maintained a natural course (of direct analogy) in their own linguistic and mental developments and remain uncontaminated by the influences of other peoples on their own language and culture. Natural growth ensures the purity and superiority of the language and culture of a community over others, while mixing of languages, mental processes and cultures renders them impure and "confounded". This process would have given rise to the great diversity of human languages and cultures.

> ... when a language is a collection of several unrelated languages, everything is confounded. Analogy can no longer make it clear in the different meanings of words, the origin and development of knowledge: we no longer know how to make our speech precise (Ibid., p. 134).

Condillac's naturalist theory of linguistic and mental development has had two consequences. One is historical and the other anthropological. The latter has to do with the firm conviction à la Sapir and Whorf (passing through Humboldt) regarding linguistic relativism/determinism: language determines thought. Therefore the existence of diverse languages suggests a diversity of stages of mental development and thinking on the basis of different degrees of analysis attained and applied. The former involves the belief that historically languages and cultures have responded differently to the original linguistic and mental disposition in man, and they would have done this in a better or a worse manner, and consequently, they would have shown correspondingly superior or inferior intellectual results in their given historical situations. This conclusion of a historical and cultural hierarchy seems to have been too facilely arrived at on the basis of the "evidence" that European scholars, aided by colonial expansions, had claimed to have obtained from the vast diversity of human languages and cultures. The great efflorescence of comparative and historical linguistics that began systematically in the fourth quarter of the 18th century (beginning with Sir William Jones, a well-paid puisne judge at the Calcutta Supreme Court and the founder of the Asiatic Society of Bengal) attests to the unprecedented philosophical and scientific interest in linguistics in the modern period.

6. Herder and the Question of the *Volk*

The first significant break with a rationalism divorced from the realm of human cultural experience took place with the works of Johann Gottfried Herder, once the most favourite students of the principal German Enlightenment philosopher Immanuel Kant. Herder, famously reneged from Kant and joined the anti-Enlightenment and proto-Romanticist movement initiated by Johann Georg Hamann, to the utter chagrin of his first mentor. Born just two years earlier than William Jones, he knew the work of the latter, especially his translation of Kalidasa's *Shankuntala*, which he is said to have recommended to Goethe. With his interest in human intellectual origins, he ushered in a philosophy of history marked by a strong sense of cultural pluralism.

With Hamann's critique of Kant and Enlightenment, the question of reconnecting man with God had already appeared. A concomitant question was the relevance of poetry and the uniqueness of each human culture. The speculation about language is no more that of its source in reason or thought, but of knowing what language God spoke and passed on to the first humans He created. This speculation has been aptly characterized by Maurice Olender as that of determining "the language of paradise." By Herder's time, there was already evidence of a diversity of rich texts and culturally significant discourses from different parts of the globe that European scholars had started to become familiar with. After Condillac had claimed that language was the foundation of human reason and thinking, what fascinated many Romanticists—who were not averse to the absolute of divinity and of poetry—was the question of the language that man spoke at the moment of his divine creation, that is, in paradise and in the cradle of the human civilization. This was important for them in the wake of the new competitors that could stake a claim to it in the wake of the European colonial expansion.

As a philosopher of history, Herder's focus was on human cultural and linguistic origins. A pastor keenly engaged in religion, his initial attention was turned to the Hebrew language, particularly Hebrew poetry. This was the time when the oriental was identified as the original. An oriental language, Hebrew of the Old Testament, for the Christians and the Jews, must be thought of as the original language. Herder is initially almost devotional towards Hebrew, assumed to be man's first language that links him with God. The poetic simplicity of the Hebrew language is considered as a virtue, for that makes it less abstract and rich in images, and thus confirming its claim to being the original language.

Herder's campaigns flourished under the influence of Georg Hamann, a wayward philosopher compared with the disciplined Kant, but yet one of the pioneering thinkers of early German Romanticism.[4] The idea of a transcendentally available universal mental disposition as posited by the Enlightenment philosophy was rejected by Hamann and his followers like Herder, who replaced it with the notion of *volkgeist* (folk spirit) that was manifested in ordinary people's language, literature, history, mythology, folktales and religion. According to Herder, humans everywhere start with the same mental capacities, but their experience of living in specific conditions and contexts, as well as their specific historical conditions, form their mentalities differently. These acquired mental dispositions, in turn, are manifested in their differential creative outputs, that is, in their languages, tales and myths, cultures and religious thoughts and beliefs.

Herder's main merit, according to many commentators, is in having favoured cultural pluralism that was indeed not devoid of features of relativism.[5] Unlike the proponents of reason on the one hand, and the votaries of divine creation on the other, Herder projected language as the decisive feature in human history and human existence. Human beings are made of languages, their nature is but "a tissue of language" (Quoted in Olender, M., 2008, p. 33). Human reason needs language to grow and articulate itself. The grammatical form of any language, whether simple or complex, reflects a people's experience of the world as impressed in language. Unlike Voltaire,[6] who as a major philosopher of Enlightenment despised the given religious texts, both Jewish and Christian, Herder in a properly Romantic vein admired Hebrew poetry for its simplicity and spiritual richness that reflected a paradisiacal innocence.

Poetry, Herder claimed, was also the mode of political organization of ancient societies. The spirit of Hebrew poetry that first appeared through Moses, manifested politically in the form of the Jewish law that God had passed on to the Prophet. The Jewish nation (*Volk*) commenced with the spiritual "sign" that God made to the people through Moses, which revealed the law that constituted the Jewish people. Thus God's word, the spirit of poetry and the language of law, all these converged in the making of this ancient *Volk.* Language is therefore not just a means for expressing the universal reason, but each nation is provided with a divine linguistic source simultaneously spiritual-poetic and legal-political, which undergoes historical developments.

Herder, as a historian of humanity, attempted to trace its progress through time in terms of the differential attainments of languages and mentalities in different nations, which were in turn the result of human interaction and sense-making. Human societies are all equally endowed and they progressed in history according to the *zeitgeist* or time-spirit of each, but at the same time, the succession of epochs in the universal human history is predetermined by the Divine plan, that is, the Christian Providence. In effect, Herder pursued the thought of a vibrant cultural pluralism, where every culture is historically progressing in terms of its own singularity, but ultimately, the whole of human history unfolds according to the Providential plan. And moreover, since each nation had its own internal developments and and destiny (though within Providential terms), Herder was opposed to any form of religious conversion. As Olender relates Herder's position: "To convert a nation to Christianity by imposing on it a new way of life is to compel it to betray its own values, to lose its own identity, and thus to imperil its spiritual and political integrity" (Ibid., p. 42).

But yet, understanding the creative unfolding of human history—even if humans are sense-making agents—is possible only as "an art of uncovering the divine order hidden in the Bible" (Ibid., p. 44). A historian, Herder would expect, to be "a prophet of the past," a poet whose work is based on an aesthetics of Providence" (Ibid., p. 44). Olender notes that if Herder subordinates a secular "cultural history respecting national and spiritual diversities" to a Lutheran "providential anthropology", that's because, for him ultimately only the Bible provides "(r)evelation in the proper sense of the word." Other religions can only provide mythology, liturgy or high morality. Herder's final *coup de grace* is directed at Judaism, whose holy scriptures, their prayers and moral judgments are "sublime writings," but in spite of that Providence itself had made a decision in favour of Christianity as the "unique design for our species" (Ibid., p. 48). Herder is ultimately dismissive of the Jews as a "parasitic plant"; and goes on to predict that they will be assimilated and will begin "to live according to European laws" (Ibid., 49, endnote, 28).

7. William Jones and the Beginnings of Colonial Linguistics

This excursus into Herder's thought was necessary in order to understand better the intricacies of William Jones' historical-civilizational propositions. A recent work on Jones has shown his dependence on an "antique theology" that undermines Jones' reputation as a liberal and progressive orientalist scholar. The Swiss author of *The Birth of Orientalism* (App 2010) Urs App's main criticism of Jones runs as follows:

> While the volumes of the *Asiatick Researches* stunned their European readership by their utterly secular and objective outlook on Asia and thus propagated a new kind of orientalism that was no more the handmaiden of theology, [William] Jones's yearly discourses show how even the erudite and coolheaded founder of the Asiatick Society remained chained to Europe's time-honored religious ideology with its peculiar vision of an extremely short history dominated by a God who kindly instructed his first creatures, drowned most of their descendants in the deluge, and had three sons of Noah populate the entire world in a couple of thousand years. While Jones's papers on a wide range of oriental subjects, his letters, and his editorship of the *Asiatick Researches* show him as a pivotal figure in the move towards orientalism's emancipation from theology, his yearly discourses demonstrate a surprisingly deep attachment to Bible-inspired chronology, sacred history, and ancient theology. Edward Said was right in stating that Jones was ideology-driven; but the nature of that ideology as well as its connection to European colonialism will have to be reevaluated (App 2009, p. 77).

According to Jones' mytho-geographical scheme outlined in the third anniversary lecture of February 2, 1786, the "vast continent" of Asia has been inherited by "five principal nations': the Hindus (Indians), the Chinese, the Tartars, the Arabs, and the Persians. His stated intention is to study them all in every detail, so that a "more perfect knowledge of them all" would be to the advantage of the Europeans (Jones 1984, p. 5). He is also interested in knowing about their common origins, if any. He begins with the study of the Indians in the third lecture "On the Hindus," because, he says, "it is the country, which we now inhabit, and from which we may best survey the regions around us" (Ibid.). His own historical description of India is decidedly partial, for he intends to keep the Muslim period out of his scholarly considerations. He says: "...in all these inquiries concerning the history of India, I shall confine my researches downwards to the Mohammedan conquests at the beginning of the eleventh century, but extend them upwards, as high as possible, to the earliest authentic records of the human species" (Ibid.).

Central to Jones' geographical-historical accounts are the following principal themes:

- the British are now in command of the Indian territory (Bengal to begin with) and are now settlers on this land;
- the Muslim rulers and their religion and culture present in the Indian territory are irrelevant for studying the history of India;
- India is the prized possession of the British, and its antiquity is directly linked with the antiquity of the Europeans;
- the Biblical (Old Testament, i.e. Mosaic) account of the history and geography of the peoples of the world can be attested by modern studies under the aegis of the Asiatic Society of Bengal that he founded in 1784;
- the British have a God-given (Providential) role to guide the destiny of the Indian people.

Thomas Trautmann has noted that Jones' civilizational project owes itself largely to what is referred to as "Mosaic ethnology" (Trautmann, T., 2006, p. 10). Mosaic ethnology has its source in the idea of the Tree of nations mentioned in the Biblical Book of Genesis, and attributed to Moses. The tree-structure indicates the descending relations of kinship among nations. According to Trautmann, "the Mosaic ethnology is a simple technology for determining the relations among peoples, conceived as branching lineages of the human family tree, as relations of far and near" (Ibid., p. 11). Significantly, Jones' claims that his modern historical studies could establish a more or less seamless mapping between the ancient Biblical accounts and the contemporary lay of the lands. In the 10th Anniversary lecture

(February 1793) Jones is explicit and even ecstatic about the discovery of the truth of the Mosaic ethnology and the role of Providence in having aided in establishing the connection between modern Britain and the antiquity of India:

> ... all our historical researches have confirmed the *Mosaick* accounts of the primitive world; and our testimony on that subject ought to have the greater weight, because, if the result of our observations had been totally different, we should nevertheless have published them, not indeed with equal pleasure, but with equal confidence; for *Truth is mighty, and,* whatever be its consequences, *must always prevail...* (Jones 1793).

And furthermore:

> In these *Indian* territories, which Providence has thrown into the arms of *Britain* for their protection and welfare, the religion, manners, and laws of the natives preclude even the idea of political freedom; but their histories may possibly suggest hints for their prosperity, while our country derives essential benefit from the diligence of a placid and submissive people, who multiply with such increase, even after the ravages of famine... (Ibid.).

Here again, Jones insists on Britain's God-given responsibility over the Indian people, and therefore the need for perpetuating the recently established colonial rule. The Mosaic ethnology is clearly articulated in Jones' 9th anniversary Discourse of February 23, 1792. As per this, the world is inhabited by the descendants of Noah's three sons *Ham*, *Sham* and *Yafet*. After the great deluge, Noah's family had initially settled down in northern Iran. Then the expanding family of the descendants of *Yafet* spread over northern Europe and Asia. They were on the whole unlettered and far from being cultured. The descendants of *Ham*, invented the letter, were good in astrology, produced an old mythology, and went on to live in the regions of Misr (Egypt), Cush (Ethiopia), other parts of Africa and India. And, the descendants of *Shem*, settled in the region now known as Middle East, consisted among others, of the Arabs, the Syrians and the Phoenicians. Jones' mythical ethnology states that the descendants of Abraham, would have come from all three families, and they are described as "bold adventurers of an ardent spirit and a roving disposition, who disdained subordination and wandered in separate clans," who began to cohere as a distinct group only about 1500 years before the beginning of the Christian era (Jones 1984, pp. 91-92).

It is also in the ninth anniversary discourse Jones makes a most unacceptable and derogatory reference to the prophet of the Muslims (Ibid., p. 83).

It is worth noting that Jones first came to India with the aim of translating into English the Persian law, which he thought was the basis of Indian society. After his discovery and learning of Sanskrit in Benares, he went on to identify this role for the text of *Manusmriti*, also known as the "Manu's laws". That for the British political authorities Jones's main scholarly contribution was to have translated this text—by now infamous for its derogatory views on the Dalits—and referred to it as the basis of the Hindu (Indian) law— and not his philological and literary outputs—is evident from the fact that in the hall of fame at St. Paul's Cathedral in London, a larger than life statue of his exists, with Jones wearing a Roman toga and holding the Book of Manu's Law, suggesting that he was the principal law-giver for British India. After Jones' death owing to a sudden liver failure in 1794, he was interred under what would be the largest European tomb in the South Park Street Cemetery in Calcutta.

The European civilizational account forcefully narrated by Sir William Jones emerged later in a full-blown manner and with more intense political ramifications, including the propagation of the Aryan myth in the 19th century. This has been submitted to an astute analysis in the work of Maurice Olender (1989/2008 edition). Historically, there has always been a yearning to name the original and perfect language of mankind. In the European context this was spoken of as the language of paradise, where man was originally united with God, and whose language was that in which God spoke to the first man, Adam. Augustine, claimed it was Hebrew, but many rejected this hypothesis, and some even suggested that the honour of being the original language went to Syriac.

William Jones' declaration on Sanskrit, its "exquisite refinement" and its possibly having come from a no longer extant common source, along with the other European classical languages, Greek and Latin, upset the hitherto dominant position of Hebrew and downgraded the status of Semitic languages in general. His strong claims in this regard, as we know, led to the hypothesis regarding an Indo-European "family" of languages, and caused a seismic shift in understanding the racial composition of Europe and the rest of the world. In the mid 19th century, after comparative and historical linguistics had been firmly established in Germany, F. Max Müller, who was made the first Chair of Comparative Philology at Oxford University, had summed up the significance of this change:

> Thanks to the discovery of the ancient language of India, Sanskrit as it is called... and thanks to the discovery of the close kinship between this language and the idioms of the principal races of Europe, which was established by the genius of Schlegel, Humboldt, Bopp, and many others, a complete revolution has taken place in the method of studying the world's primitive history (Quoted in Olender 1989, p. 7).

The twists and turns in the conceptions of world history between 1750 and 1850 must be stated more specifically in terms of the fluctuating fortunes of Hebrew and Sanskrit, by then, the two main contenders or being the "languages of paradise."[7] As early as the 1750s the principal French Enlightenment philosopher Voltaire, was keen to detach the European civilization from its Biblical-religious, and Hebrew origins, and look for alternatives, possibly from the shores of the Ganges in India. Along with the discovery of Vedic texts and with the beginning of the colonial domination of the Indian subcontinent, an "Aryan" paradise was considered to supersede the Adamic Hebrew paradise.

8. Humboldt: Typology, National Character and the Race Hierarchy

By the time Wilhelm von Humboldt had written his major philological works and died in 1835, comparative and historical linguistics had come of age through the efforts of Franz Bopp, the Schlegel brothers and others. Humboldt as a philosopher-cum-philologist who carried the traits of early 19th century philosophy of history inherited from Herder, was acquainted with philological analysis, and was sympathetic to the Romanticist literary-philosophical movement. His main contribution in what he and others had set up as a philosophy of language is two-fold: *a.* to firm up the idea of a genealogical classification of world's languages in terms of a family-tree model, and *b.* even more importantly to propose a classification of the world's languages in terms of linguistic structure or morphology. Unlike Herder, Humboldt partially adopted Kantian rationalism and was also "scientifically" inclined. For him, there is a mental capacity specific to language as such, the ideal "inner linguistic sense" which interacts with the material phonetic part in diverse ways, depending on the effort or energy expended by the speakers of particular languages, to yield a diversity of languages. In Humboldt's conception, there is a potential ideal of such a combination, but which perhaps no language really attains. Depending on how well a linguistic community has worked on their language, the linguistic structures have appeared that are more or less perfect. If the genealogical typology shows merely the historical relationships among languages and their classification in terms of family relationships, the morphological typology reveals a scale of structural perfection of different families of languages and their members have attained with regard to the ideal combination of the universal mental component of language ("inner linguistic sense") and the limited human sound forms. This structural hierarchy is headed by the Indo-European languages of the ancient period, which manifest an *inflectional* morphological type. These languages (Sanskrit, Greek and Latin) have structures that approximate to what in Humboldt's view involve an ideal melding of external sound and inner linguistic sense. They are followed by the other structural types of languages, the agglutinating, isolating and incorporating types, in that hierarchal order.

Humboldt's linguistic and concomitantly racial biases are evident in the following statement:

> We have everywhere set out at first from the *structure* of languages alone, and in forming a judgement about it have also confined ourselves

> solely to this. Now that this structure is better in one than another, is more excellent in Sanskrit than in Chinese, and in Greek than in Arabic, could hardly be disputed by any impartial scholar. However we might try to weigh off their respective virtues, we should always have to admit that one of these languages is animated by a *more fruitful principle of mental development* than the other.

The structural superiority is construed on the belief that in the making of the ancient Indo-European inflectional languages, the speakers have spent more intellectual energy in the internal structural formation of the roots to yield diverse forms, whereas in languages like Chinese or Arabic, grammatical variations are merely a matter of differing word-orders or morphological suffixing respectively. In Humboldt's view, what makes the latter linguistically inferior is the fact no conscious linguistic thought was employed to get morphological and grammatical variations by means of root-inflections. And, correspondingly and by extension, as many philologists believed, a poorer grammatical formation is an indication of lesser intellectual development, and hence the "evident" superiority of the Indo-European languages with inflections over the Semitic (e.g. Hebrew and Arabic) and the Dravidian languages which have agglutinating structures, and over the Sino-Tibetan family of languages with their isolating structures. This hierarchy is thus assumed to be correlated with their racial status.

Humboldt's account of race-based nationalism is equally complex. Though like Kant and other rationalists, he accepted that all humans have the same initial mental make-up, according to Humboldt during the primitive formation of their languages, the inner linguistic sense combined with the sound form, rather unconsciously, in a single burst of energy, as it were, which guided the destiny of languages and their families. Thus, it is no more Providence that is responsible for the racial superiority or inferiority, but a chance spontaneous occurrence that privileged certain nations and their languages, but not others in their subsequent intellectual and linguistic development. Once this mysterious event had taken place, the language and the mentality of different peoples moved along their predestined courses in forming their inexorable "national characters." It is this inexplicable mental-linguistic event that determines the superiority of certain nations and races (e.g. the Indo-Europeans) over the others (e.g. the Semitics, the Chinese, etc.).

9. Max Müller and the 'Natural Selection' of Languages

Max Müller is perhaps the most curious figure in the history of modern linguistics. Starting off as a student of the comparatist Franz Bopp in Berlin, he went on to become the first Chair of Comparative Philology at Oxford University. By that time the "Aryan" race and religion and the Sanskrit language have been raised to an exalted position in European scholarship. Müller began his career with the intent of founding a Science of Religion, but simultaneously he invented a historicist and positivist Science of Language. That he is indeed one of the most venerated European scholars in India, is evident from the fact that a most prestigious street in central New Delhi is named after him. However, it is worth noting that his enthusiasm for everything Sanskrit, Aryan, Hindu and Indo-European led him to make an odd claim in a report submitted to the British army. Trautmann points out that:

> Max Müller said, in 1854, that the same blood flowed in the veins of the soldiers of (Robert) Clive that flowed in the veins of the "dark Bengalese," and that this truth, contrary to the testimony of skin color, was guaranteed by the linguistic connection between English and Bengali as members of the same Indo-European language family. (1854: 29)[8] Thus language, not complexion, is a sign of the inner and invisible entity called race and symbolized by blood (Trautmann, 2006, pp. 221-22).

Race and religion were central concerns for Max Müller as well as for his French interlocutor and historian Ernest Renan. But, for the former, both race and religion were intimately related to language. Against Renan's view that the Jews had developed an instinct for monotheism, Müller argued that soon after God's act of creation, a divine intuition was implanted in man by way of a revelation. This intuition, we should imagine was something like an "inner religious sense", perhaps akin to Humboldt's inner linguistic sense, and the former varied "according to the expression which it took in the languages of man[9] Therefore divergence of human languages was a consequence of how the revealed divinity was expressed differently in different languages. The task of the new science of language that he proposed was to investigate the primordial link between divinity and languages. In Müller's words, "(t)he history of religion is, in one sense the history of language" (Ibid., p. 84).

The question of religion and that of language converged in Müller on the notion of linguistic "roots" (note that this is a prominent notion in Sanskrit grammatical texts) as distinct from the earlier major notion of "signs". It served him in distinguishing the animal from the human, the natural from the cultural-mythological and finally, Judaic monotheism from Aryan polytheism. Working backwards in the history of linguistic roots, Müller went on to claim that it is the roots having a primordial divine content, which separated the beasts from men, and the natural from the religious-mythological. He also identified the distinction between the agglutinating Semitic type of language and the inflecting Aryan type of language as the distinction of how their respective roots functioned. The Semitic roots are easily identifiable, and therefore their substantial meanings can be taken to be transparent. This simplicity of the Semitic roots wherein the natural and the divine could be kept separate is what renders these languages more prone to monotheism. While in the Aryan languages, the roots are mired and become indistinct in a complex inflectional system of suffixes and derivations that such a transparent relationship between them and the natural world could not exist, and therefore the roots of words are easily transfigured from the natural domain to the transcendental. Thus, for example, the "sun" can easily be transposed as God in the Aryan languages, a pattern that results in rich but often misleading mythological formations. The task of a science of language, for Müller, was to dig deep into language past the level where the mythological obscures the level of the roots and where divine intuition is inexorably merged with the most primordial "roots" of human languages. However, it must be noted, as Olender points out, that Müller's sense of linguistic-religious cosmopolitanism did not prevent him from insisting on the uniqueness and superiority of Christianity in the Providential order of which he was aware perhaps in the same manner as Herder (Ibid., pp. 90-92).

At the peak of his career in the mid 19th century, Müller was also deeply influenced, as by both Darwin's evolutionary theory (mediated by the work of August Schleicher[10]: *Darwinist Theory and the Language Science*) and the positivist philosophy of Auguste Comte. It can be seen that Müller was, along positivist lines "rationalizing" the social or the conventional part of language. And moreover, it is biological evolution that makes languages historically more and more rational. Languages and language forms, in their own historical existence, undergo an evolutionary selection, akin to biological selection as proposed by Darwin. Perhaps, Max Müller expressed this idea more forcefully than Darwin himself had wished, and the latter openly acknowledged Müller's contribution in showing language as the best instance of how his own evolutionary theory works. After crediting Epicurus for suggesting the idea of (social) convention alongside with the natural part of language, Müller states:

> Let us substitute for this Epicurean idea of a conventional agreement an idea which did not exist in his time, and the full elaboration of which in our own time we owe to the genius of Darwin; —let us place instead of agreement, *Natural Selection,* or, as I called it in my former Lectures, *Natural Elimination,* and we shall then arrive, I believe, at an understanding with Epicurus, and even with some of his modern followers (Quoted in Harris and Taylor 1997, p. 183).

The laws for the positivistically-inclined linguistics of the mid-19th century are no longer divine laws passed on to man through a prophet as it was for Herder. They are now historical laws akin to the biological laws as required by the methodological tenets of positivism. Müller invokes what seems like a Kantian epistemological imperative to speak of the reason behind a Darwinian kind of natural evolution of languages.

General notions are not formed at random, but according to law, that law being our reason within corresponding to the reason without—to the reason, if I may so call it, of nature. Natural selection, if we could but always see it, is invariably rational selection (Quoted in Ibid., p. 184).This would mean that it was not Providence that guided the forward movement of the world's languages, but a biological principle of natural selection, or expressed in more savage terms, the survival of the rationally fit. Therefore, it is an intrinsic mental process of functional-qualitative selection that has favoured the surviving languages. Or, those languages that have survived are to be deemed as the best! The forms that have disappeared were not fit to survive. We do not know if Max Müller was aware of the irony of his statement, for from another perspective it is those so-called languages that were dead and disappeared in ancient times were the one's which were supposed to have a philologically robust structure, at least from the Humboldtian perspective mentioned earlier.

Of course, Max Müller would have eventually compromised his biblical idea of linguistic creation implying a metaphysical division between animal and human languages, with the Darwinian idea of the survival of the fittest linguistic forms along the evolutionary ladder. Along the lines of the positivistically-oriented "Neogrammarians" of the second half of the 19th century, Müller would argue that language change involved the "selection" and survival of those forms that emerged randomly but which had higher functional value. In other words, there is an intrinsic evolutionary reason for languages to undergo changes. Harris and Taylor have noted that,

> Müller's originality lies in his attempt to graft a Darwinian concept of evolution on to a Cartesian linguistic stock. He invokes the 'faculty of reason' *(logos),* unique to *Homo sapiens,* as the explanation for how human beings (unlike parrots) were able to make the unprecedented evolutionary leap from calls to words, from spontaneous chatter to deliberate language (Ibid., p. 192).

10. Structuralism and the Making of 20th Century Linguistics

Having been trained in the milieu of the Neogrammarians, the Swiss scholar Ferdinand de Saussure, inherited many of the tenets of his teachers of the German school. However, his later posthumous work

Cours de linguistique générale of 1916 also marked the beginning of the end of the dominance of the European tradition of historical linguistics or philology that reigned for more than a century. Saussure's break with that tradition also implied for him a decisive break with Positivism. He rejected the notion of a continuous movement of physical linguistic material which undergoes historical changes on the basis of laws that are akin to biological laws in the natural order. Linguistic entities, in his view, cannot be understood other than as parts of a holistic system. For Saussure, the notion of a system or structure has relevance both in the context of the people who speak a given language and for the system of interconnected elements of that language. At the beginning of the 20th century, his role was to take language outside the prevailing framework of naturalist explanations for changes in individual elements, albeit according to laws, and instead to provide an alternative perspective where language is seen as embedded within a living social (and psychological) milieu.

One of Saussure's central innovations was to reintroduce the traditional notion of the "sign". But, he gives a radically new definition of the sign, different from what had prevailed during the ancient, medieval or early modern periods. His "sign" integrates the formal and the meaning parts into a single undivided unit without privileging either. Furthermore, a sign can only exist as part of an integral system of signs. Saussure does not see words or other linguistic elements as having independent natural—physical or biological—existence, but they can exist only as parts of an autonomous system. Linguistic elements or signs can exist only relationally and systemically. And furthermore, they do not exist so only for any particular individual, but only in the psychological states of all the members of a given social collectivity. Language, for him is thus a "doubly holistic system", without the possibility of any physical continuity in time. This idea is the basis of Saussure's well-known dichotomy between the diachronic and the synchronic modes of analysis, where the former cannot be undertaken without resorting to independent synchronic analyses of a language at different points of time. The synchronic system that never physically manifests as such, is for Saussure, the main object of linguistic study.

But the language system is a quasi-psychological reality that exists in a biological (in its formation) and mechanical (in its functioning) modes which are part of the social reality. This is evident from Saussure's characterization of Semiology (of which linguistics would be a branch) as "a science that studies the life of signs at the core of social life" (Saussure, 1959, p. 16). It is some sort of an organic and unconscious mental system that is simultaneously present in the mind/brain of every individual of a society, who speaks a language. Signs arise bio-mechanically in the brain by way of a chance bonding of their meaning (signified) and formal (signifier) sides, which belong respectively to a nebulous thought stream and an "equally chaotic" realm of sounds. Thus, for Saussure, language is 'a form, and not substance.' Structurally, this would entail that language is not yet made up of traces of phonetic or psychological substances, but it is made up of differences, "differences without positive terms," as per his well-known formulation. And furthermore, even though these differences may have the potential of introducing changes or alterations in language, by way of change in the "values" of terms in the series of sounds and meanings, that would still be mainly formal and mechanical processes in which the language-users play only a limited role. The enigma of language in Saussure's formulation is that it cannot be changed consciously and it can also not remain the same.

While trying to set up an autonomous linguistics, we notice that Saussure has subtracted from his system of language the role of the living individual, of historical time, of community and of real substances, phonetic or psychological. This has been the bane of linguistic structuralism, present more starkly in the two varieties of American structuralism, viz. Bloomfieldian distributionalism and Sapir and Whorf's anthropological linguistics. The former has its theoretical model derived from behaviouristic psychology, where formalism reigns and meaning is relegated as the "weak point of language-study" (Bloomfield 1980, p. 140). This is because if meanings can be studied, it is only by considering them as physical stimuli that correspond to the linguistic responses in the behaviourist sense. While, in the Sapir-Whorf perspective, meaning is meant to have a cultural significance, especially with respect to the Hopi, Maya and other native Indian languages, but that assertion is intended to show the superiority, in an anthropological sense, of the cognitive correlates of their grammatical forms vis-à-vis those of what Whorf referred to as Standard Average European (SAE). The day-to-day, lived linguistic transactions that the natives were engaged in remained outside the scope of their anthropological linguistic theory.

11. Contemporary Scene: After Structuralism

Linguistics (proper) in the second half of the 20th century has been dominated by mentalist approaches initiated by Noam Chomsky. His early work was prompted by the question of computational (mechanical) processing of any and every human language. This was accompanied by a stringent critique of behaviourism (of Skinner and Bloomfield) in linguistic studies. This has of course resulted in the treatment of language as an objective system, much more than what Saussure had envisaged. This system is furthermore regarded as innate and mental (in the sense of neurologically embedded). The object of Chomskyan analysis is the linguistic competence of an "ideal speaker-hearer" who can generate indefinitely many grammatically correct sentences. Chomsky had claimed during the mid-1960s the affiliation of his method and theory, however dubious, to Cartesian rationalism, and related psychological models. Since then he has however shifted his interest to biological, i.e. neurological explanations of language. Though he is also a well-known political commentator against authoritarian governmental practices anywhere especially in the US, his politics and his linguistics have remained markedly divergent from the very beginning of his exceptionally famous academic career.

The other approach, popularly known as "post-structuralism", was even more critical of Structuralism. The post-structuralist philosophers, Deleuze, Foucault and Derrida have approached the question of language as part of their interest in reversing the Enlightenment philosophies and have been openly political. Of these, while Foucault tried to account for the transformations in the linguistic domain on the basis of long-term shifts in discursive formations (as briefly discussed in Section 3 above), Deleuze and Derrida have brought politics into the very core of their linguistic theories in order to challenge the essentialist philosophies of language that had prevailed from Socrates to Saussure. Derrida has questioned the "metaphysics of presence" that lies at the very core of much of the philosophical positions on language. Deleuze has sought to induce a new philosophical pragmatics of language that is fundamentally political. Countering much of Rationalist and Romanticist positions on language, which were intended to *construct* systems of knowledge and discourses, these philosophers have adopted methods that involve the opposite: *discontinuity and* (power-discourse) *genealogy* (Foucault), *différance* and *deconstruction* (Derrida) and *deterritorialisation* (Deleuze). We can only briefly refer to the most salient aspects of the Poststructuralist movement within the scope of the present paper.

Both Deleuze and Derrida have, in their own ways, rejected the traditional notion of the "sign" and the associated accounts of static and invariable meanings. Derrida's alternative proposals regarding *trace*, *différance* and *supplement* are aimed to seek a profound deconstruction of the "sign". While, Deleuze has insisted on a non-communicational pragmatic ordering of the world in and by language, which in his view, must be reversed. Suggesting a directly political understanding of language studies, Deleuze and Guattari avow that "(p)ragmatics is a politics of language" (Deleuze and Guattari 1987, p. 82).

Perhaps, the most significant work in recent times that address the political dimensions of language in the context of nationalism and colonialism has been Derrida's *Monolingualism of the Other—OR, The Prosthesis of Origin.* Here there is a sensitive analysis of the key question of identity in and through language presented through accounts from his personal experiences. He goes on to ask the question: Can one really own a language? Who determines (politically) the main features of one's language? Derrida begins to reflect on these issues an oxymoronic statement: "I have only one language; but it is not mine." Elsewhere in the work, he demonstrates the colonial character of all language as long as it is situated within a "culture":

> All culture is originally colonial.... Every culture institutes itself through the unilateral imposition of some "politics" of language. Mastery begins as we know, through the power of naming, of imposing and legitimating appellations. We know how that went with France in France itself, in revolutionary France as much as or more than, in monarchical France. This sovereign establishment may be open, legal, armed, or cunning, disguised under the alibis of "universal" humanism, and sometimes of the most generous hospitality. It always follows or precedes culture like its shadow (Derrida 1998, p. 59).

NOTES

1. Jean-Pierre Vernant has noted: "Scientific rationality defines itself as it constructs the subject matter and methodology of each new discipline. In the human science, moreover, there is no virgin territory to explore; the fields of investigation are continents mapped by tradition and explored by religious thought." (in Olender 2008, pp. viii-ix)
2. Foucault refers to the publication in Petersburg, Russia, in 1787 the first volume of the *Camparitivum Totius Orbis* which "include references to 279 languages; 171 in Asia, 55 in Europe, 30 in Africa, 23 in America." This was possibly the largest comparative glossary of world's languages based on the notion of a basic vocabulary. (Ibid., p. 234)
3. "Inflection" is a grammatical mode where verbal morphology is based on the internal changes of the root. For example, "buy" → "brought", or "bring" → "brought" as distinct from "work" → "worked". The languages which have "inflection" as their major mode of verbal morphology were traditionally referred to as "inflectional languages" (e.g. Sanskrit, Greek and Latin), as distinct from the "agglutinating" languages where grammatical elements are added on the root (e.g. Turkish, Hebrew, Tamil), and the "isolating" languages, where the roots and grammatical elements remain unconnected (e.g. Chinese).
4. Frederick Beiser says of Hamann: "It is difficult to exaggerate the many respects in which Hamann influenced the *Sturm and Drang,* and ultimately Romanticism itself. The metaphysical significance of art, the importance of the artist's personal vision, the irreducibility of cultural difference, the value of folk poetry, the social and historical dimension of rationality, and the significance of language for thought—all these themes were prevalent in, or characteristic of, the *Sturm und Drang*

and Romanticism. But they were first adumbrated by Hamann, and then elaborated and promulgated by Herder, Goethe, and Jacobi." (Beiser 1987, p. 16)

5. See Maurice Olender 1998. Olender devotes a full chapter to Herder (pp. 37-50).
6. It is said of Voltaire that he attacked Judaism in order to hit even harder at Christianity.
7. Olender justifies the title and the contents of his book thus: "The sources on which this book is based invite us to consider Aryans and Semites as functional pair with a providential aspect, as elements of a theory of the origins..." (Ibid., p. 18) The dramatic story of the origin and development of civilization (as described by Ernest Renan) reads follows: "Aryan and Semite: "two twins" at the origin of civilization. Discovered in the "same cradle," they constitute a pair with unequal virtues [inset quotes are from Renan]. Separated in early childhood, Aryans and Semites follow singular destinies, are distinct in every way. In a divine drama whose theatre is universal history, Providence sees to it that each plays its proper role. The Aryans bring the West mastery over nature, exploitation of time and space, the invention of mythology, science, and art, but the Semites hold the secret of monotheism—at least that fateful day when Jesus comes into the world at Galilee." (Ibid., pp. 13-14)
8. Müller, M, *Suggestions for the Assistance of Officers in Learning the Languages of the Seat of War in the East.* London: Williams and Norgate. 1854. Referred in Trautmann 2006, p. 191.
9. Quoted in Olender 2008, p. 83., from Max Müller's *New Lessons on the Science of Language* (1863),
10. A. Schleicher: "Grammar is a branch of linguistics or glottics. This in turn is a component of the Natural History of Man. Their characteristic method is that of the natural sciences ... One of the key tasks of glottics is the classification and description of groups of dialects or linguistic branches, that is to say, languages derived from a single and even original language, and the classification of these branches following a natural order." (My translation of a citation in the French Wikipedia: « *La grammaire est une branche de la linguistique ou* glottique. *Celle-ci est à son tour une composante de l'histoire naturelle de l'Homme. Leur méthode caractéristique est celle des sciences naturelles... L'une des tâches essentielles de la glottique est le classement et la description des groupes de parlers, ou des rameaux linguistiques, c'est-à-dire des langues dérivant d'une seule et même langue originelle, et la classification de ces rameaux suivant un ordre naturel* » (Schleicher, A. 2014)

REFERENCES

Anderson, Benedict, *Imagined Communities: Reflections on the Origin and Spread of Nationalism* (London: Verso, 1991edn.).

App, Urs, *The Birth of Orientalism* (Philadelphia: University of Pennsylvania Press, 2010).

App, Urs, "William Jones' Ancient Theology" in *Sino-Platonic Papers* 191 (online edn.) (2009/2008), p. 77.

Beiser, Frederick C., *The Fate of Reason: German Philosophy from Kant to Fichte* (Harvard: Harvard University Press, 1987).

Bloomfield, Leonard, *Language (*Delhi: Motilal Banarsidass, 1980 edn).

Cohn, Bernard S., *Colonialism and its Forms of Knowledge: The British in India (*Delhi: Oxford University Press, 1996).

Deleuze, Gilles and Felix Guattari, *A Thousand Plateaus: Capitalism and Schizophrenia,* trans. B. Massumi (Minneapolis: University of Minnesota Press, 1987).

Derrida, Jacques, *Monolingualism of the Other OR, The Prosthesis of Origin,* trans. P. Mensard (Stanford: Stanford University Press, 1998).

Errington, Joseph J., *Linguistics in a Colonial World: A Story of Language, Meaning, and Power* (Oxford: Blackwell, 2008).

Foucault, Michel, *Order of Things: An Archaeology of the Human Sciences* (London: Tavistock, 1970).

Harrris, Roy and Talbot J. Taylor, *Landmarks in Linguistic Thought I: The Western Tradition from Socrates to Saussure* (2nd edition) (London: Routledge, 1997).

Jones, William Sir, 10th Anniversary Discourse Source: www.elohs.unifi.it/testi/700/jones/Jones_Discourse_10.html (February 1793), accessed on 24 May 2013.

Jones, Sir William, *Discourses and Essays,* M. Bagchee (ed.), *(*New Delhi: People's Publishing House, 1984).

Olender, Maurice, *The Languages of Paradise: Race, Religion, and Philology in the Nineteenth Century,* trans. A. Goldhammer (Cambridge, Mass.: Harvard University Press, 2008 edn.).

Said, Edward, *Orientalism* (New York: Vintage, 1979).

Saussure, F. de, *Course in General Linguistics*, trans. W. Baskin (New York: Philosophical Library, 1959 edn.).

Schleicher, A., Compendium der vergleichenden Grammatik (http:// fr.wikipedia.org/wiki/August_Schleicher, accessed on 24th June, 2014)

Trautmann, Thomas R., *Languages and Nations: The Dravidian Proof in Colonial Madras* (New Delhi: Yoda Press, 2006).

6

Beyond Protective Discoloration: Ambedkar on Conversion

Soumyabrata Choudhury

The thesis which I want to present in this paper is the following: The distinctive contribution that B.R. Ambedkar made to the question of conversion, which hitherto had been dominantly presented as a politico-theological question, was to clarify it with a new tool of thought. This tool was a complexly articulated *theory of names.* I would like to argue that only upon a sufficient appreciation of this theory of names, in all its semiotic, pragmatic and ontological richness, will we be able to grasp the implications of this theory for the historical terrain upon which they worked their effects. Only then can we undertake further the more perilous, and surely more urgent task of moving from Ambedkar *on* conversion to *Ambedkar's* conversion.

Such is our limited mandate: to perform the melancholy exercise of internalizing a set of abstractions that make a theory so as to enable the perilous tracking of a threshold, or maybe several sub-thresholds, of *decision.* From the desolate empire of meaning to the vibrant life of a wound: such is the intelligibility promised to our labours. But surely this was not the case with Ambedkar himself! Nothing was promised—and nothing needed to be promised—to Ambedkar in the shape of the compensation for his theoretical labours with some sort of historical fulfilment of vital destiny because at every point,

Ambedkar's decisions were as much *decisions of thought* as decisions of life. In thinking he was already intervening in the plan of destiny and in that wounding caesura of thought, setting up for himself the existential challenge of living *without destiny.* I think Ambedkar understood this challenge to be one of living a true 'political' life—and we can extrapolate from this that all the force of tragedy that invests his life does not essentially dislodge the core of Ambedkar as a *political* and *non-tragic* thinker.

Let me illustrate the above point. The essay that I am going to mainly read here for the purpose of reporting Ambedkar's theory of names as a useful perspective on conversion, the essay called "Away from the Hindus", has three dimensions (Ambedkar 1989b, pp. 403-21). The first internal dimension is an evaluative one which arises from the theoretical expedient of what abstract parameters will the "convert" choose, theological, political, pertaining to some general philosophy of religion, etc., to make her act meaningful and justifiable. The first dimension passes into the second one because the question of justification is posed within a *polemical* milieu—which means that the test is in lively interaction with a host of interlocutors, some of whom are hostile and intent on proving the cause of conversion absurd if not damaging. But the third dimension is the most concrete one because it redirects the theoretical gaze and the polemical attitude towards the historical moment of a *decision*. The theoretical expedient and the polemical fury are only epiphenomena of the declaration by the Mahar community at a conference in 1936 at Bombay that it will henceforth abandon Hinduism and be open to conversion to some other religion (Ibid., p. 403). Expressed as a formal resolution this decision is neither theoretical nor polemical; it is concrete and true. And in a way everything that follows in Ambedkar's essay, with its theatre of speculative warfare with the hostile Hindu and analytical contest with the secular sceptic, assume their real place in the light of the *affirmation* of the Mahar decision. This decision is not sunk into the solitary interiority of any one individual, even if that interiority be as fabulous as Ambedkar's own. Rather it issues from the *popular solitude* of the Mahar who lives in the clamorous world seeking the minimum access to other forms of speech, body, thought and being.[1] This amounts to say that Ambedkar's essay, at every point, affirms the affirmation of Mahars who seek a *new form of the world in the world* (Zelliot 2013, p. 150).[2]

I realize that the above has a ring of emancipatory dogma to it and anticipates the ontological horizon of conversion which, methodologically speaking, should be reserved for a later stage of the unfolding of the argument. However, I readily commit this infraction to distinguish the specialized investigators' limited scope of analytic rigour and synthetic judgment—in that order—from Ambedkar's situation of theory. Like any situation, Ambedkar's theory is plunged in syntheses of forces, one of which could well be a unilateral, undemonstrated, in that sense, 'natural-axiomatic' emancipatory force. In other words, it is no mere utopia for which I deliberately let loose my 'scientific' reins but for the *force* which the specialist must recognize as irreducible and yet acknowledge as the 'milieu' which perpetually pre-exists the separation of thought and act, theory and application. In terms of the historical reference mentioned earlier, we must not—in our reading—intervene in, and we must not also ever neglect, the historical fact that even as a "theory of conversion" was on its way, whether created by philosophers, theologians or by a thinker without destiny like Ambedkar, *there was always already conversion.*[3] There was always already conversion, *whether in thought or deed.*

Before I go on to the following section where I read parts of the essay "Away from the Hindus", I am obliged to make a clarification. Lest it be misunderstood that I privilege the greater materiality of Ambedkar's situation over the so-called specialist's dull and neutral "discipline", I must state that specialization *is* the specialist's situation. And indeed the material specificity of specialization doesn't exhaust the "person" of the specialist—and she could well be swept up by "other" passions, more popular, more solitary, more enigmatic combinations of both. My intention was to suggest that the specialist occupies an interesting but narrow precipice separating the *materiality* of a 'milieu' from the *objectivity* of a "form".[4] And by the dull—but sacred!—duty of the specialist, she must insist on the separation. And at the same time be the still wind, the connecting tissue, the sacrificial mediator keeping the two zones in disparate contact.

A Reading of Ambedkar's "Away from the Hindus" in Six Parts

Milieu

This essay—which is also a chapter from a manuscript discovered after Ambedkar's death—is written in the context of the Mahar Conference in Bombay in 1936. We know about Ambedkar's announcement on October 13, 1935 at Yeola near Nasik that he "will not die a Hindu".[5] We also know of the cancellation of Ambedkar's address at Lahore in 1936 by the Jat-Pat Todak Mandal because of its threatened declaration of leaving Hinduism. This address, published as the classic text "Annihilation of Caste", drew criticism from Gandhi to which Ambedkar replied (Ambedkar 1989a, pp. 5-16). In the present reading, however, I will keep to the letter of the essay/chapter "Away from the Hindus". Ambedkar starts out by talking of the Bombay conference but he narrates this as a proof of the Untouchable's *capacity* to deliberate, think and reach a decision to abandon Hinduism. What is the nature of such a decision?

Clearly this is not a decision to convert. It opens up the possibility of a future conversion in the most undetermined way by determining to abandon Hinduism. Hence is the strangely indeterminate yet highly determinate use of the word "away" in the title "Away from the Hindus". It is as if everything is distributed between the modalities of abandonment, a future conversion and the continuous life— which is also an infinite horizon—of "being-away" from that which has been abandoned. It is the ceaseless abandoning of that which is abandoned, the continuous revocation of what has been revoked.[6] As a contiguous milieu of Ambedkar's text, it is an infinite "deciding" of what has been decided that characterizes the historical vigilance of the Mahars and the Untouchables; it is as much their revolutionary "virtuality". But this is exactly the point at which we must arrest our reading to say that Ambedkar's stakes are not merely in the generalized emancipation of a "virtuality" or a "capacity" but in the *actual* intervention that the Untouchable-Mahar decision effectuates in the fabric of historical being. At the same time he will not overstep the very caesura that the "abandoning decision" produces in history. He will not anticipate the conjuncture of 1956 when the material of a milieu and the objectivity of a form will be fused in the decision to become Buddhist *and to write the book of this fusion itself – the Buddha and his Dhamma.*[7] I think at the time Ambedkar is writing "Away from the Hindus", he utilizes the time of caesura to "convert" it into the tool of thought which is *theory*. A whole series of theoretical virtualities to syncopate with the virtuality of a tremendous affirmation of the time of caesura on behalf of the Mahar-Untouchables : such is Ambedkar's contribution in "Away from the Hindus" of which a theory of names is a concise, lucid and interesting example.

Name

In a way I am reading the chapter backwards. Upon a thesis on the "event of the new name" that marks conversion we confront the demand of the new name to be incorporated into a commensurately new collective body. Such a collective body solicits the inner rational inner structure which Ambedkar calls "kinship" that the Untouchables seek to enter into.[8] Only when this kind of a "thinkable form" is accessible to us, we can rise to the level of an *ontology* which prescribes universalization and equalization of "life-values" that every human institution, including (and specially) religion, must follow. As a post-script to this inverted architectonic, we can extract from Ambedkar a kind of calculus of "moral use" of religion and only such *use* justifies religious belonging, neither theology nor ritual practices, not even the passion and pulsation of faith.

I speak of an inverted architectonic in the above because in Ambedkar's own construction, the ontological prescription comes first. It is a prescription towards fundamental equality which is *applied* to "life" and the "value" which is produced out of this contact. Religion must universalize this "value" to be acceptable and promissory. Then he employs a substantial amount of anthropological material to propose an internal structure for the "form" of this universalization. This structure is pivotally dependent on the element of kinship – with the extraordinary twist that kinship whose model is the 'natural' family based on descent, in the case of conversion, must be the unforeseen knot that ties together in a *non-natural, non-descensional* way, the Stranger, which the Untouchable has been forced to become, to strangers who arrive with unforeseen communities.[9] Only when Ambedkar has imagined such a sequence of untyings and re-tyings of bodies and forms does he come to the extremely localized and singular operation of the giving and taking of new names. My contention is that this concrete localized operation, over all its analytic and synthetic dimensions, does not ever cease to gaze out at the non-localizable, yet indubitably real, "scene" of the encounter between the Stranger and the strangers.

Now let us go through the stages of the operation of the name. The first stage consists of Ambedkar's hard-headed, even dry, rebuttal of the exalted attitude that views the name as a dispensable externality—a view expressed by Shakespeare's poetry ("a rose by any other name would smell as sweet...") (Ambedkar 1989b, p. 419). *But it is the name of the Untouchable that stinks!* All options of calling the Untouchable by another name are foreclosed by the historico-social violence of imposing a "generic name"—Untouchable—which collapses all particulars—all the jâti names—into its stinking genericity. This is of course the eventual material criticism of the Shakespearean aristocracy of unbound fragrances; it is also the essence of Ambedkar's refutation of Gandhi's inflexible insistence on "change of heart" as the guidepost of true converts. Neither the smell nor the heart of a rose, neither its melody nor its gospel is the real issue for Ambedkar.[10] The *real* of the question of conversion arises from the material effects of the apparent generic neutrality of a name—"Untouchable". The name's "incorporeal body" which is incorporated into the sensorium of the world as a stink and an ignominy gives the lie to its neutral form.[11]

The accompanying move in the operation of the name by Ambedkar is methodological, but with tremendous critical implications. A name is a "symbol" standing for a common platform that gathers varied particular instances and saves the subject "examination" of the *singular case* (Ambedkar 1989b, p. 419). This pragmatic economizer when returned to real history is revealed to be a *mask*, a pseudo-common name, the caste-name as it were, of an actually fragmented dispersion of "unsocial" individuals. Hindu society is in actuality, a non-society, which caste-names mark and mask as immemorially given forms of conviviality, kinship and law. But the really demystifying implication of Ambedkar's pragmatic point is that the denominalist practice of Untouchability, wearing the simpler mask of the "common name" and the more inscrutable and "neutral" one (a Noh mask!) of the "generic name" is a singular case of historical usurpation of bodies, peoples and denominations. The caste-abduction of the anthropological performativity of names that are channelized through lines of kinship is a *historical singularity.*[12] And so far as Hindu (non) society refuses to recognize the logic of this historical singularity behind the (iron) curtain of a so-called "common name" (which, according to Ambedkar, is also an endogamous closure), it is up to the Untouchable's own actual intervention into its historical arrest to free this logic and make the counter-move of an "other" name.

One counter-move the Untouchables make is the move of "protective discoloration". Illustrating the move first, Ambedkar writes: "There is a general attempt to call themselves by some name other than the 'Untouchables'. The Chamars call themselves Ravidas or Jatavas. The Doms call themselves Shilparars. The Pariahs call themselves Adi-Dravidas, the Madigas call themselves Arundhatyas, The Mahars call themselves Chokamela, or Somavamshi and the Bhangis call themselves Balmikis. All of them if away from their localities would call themselves Christians"(Ibid.). Following this extraordinary scenario where historical actuality is pregnant with the scandal of a *new genericity* (which Christian stands for in the citation and I will explain), Ambedkar writes, "The Untouchables know that if they call themselves Untouchables they will at once draw the Hindu out and expose themselves to his wrath and his prejudice. That is why they give themselves other names which may be likened to the process of undergoing protective discoloration" (Ibid).

Everything in the above is concentrated in the *localization* and *manifestation* of the name. What space of belonging does a name attest, what mode of being does it manifest? Localization and manifestation are the two features that account for names as operators of discernibility. But the terrible paradox is that the Untouchable is *too discernible*, belongs *too much* to Hindu (non)society, is *too manifest* in her mode of being whose colours are as degraded as they are vivid. Hence the search for camouflage like that of a threatened creature exposed to predation, the search for "protective discoloration" of Being endangered by Recognition so as to *become indiscernible.* Against the great subaltern narratives of "other" names of history, other depths of belonging and modes of discernment, Ambedkar reads "Ravidas", "Shilpararas", "Chokhamela", "Balmiki", etc. as tactical decisions under the pressure of circumstances and conditioned by their immanent demands.[13] Ideally if the chain of conditions—which means the state of belonging to Hindu(non)society—could be broken then the Untouchables would truly have *got away*, decisively escaped to that zero-degree of localization from where a new generic name can be decided and adopted. Ambedkar calls this name "Christian".

This is the point at which we come upon a most interesting problem in Ambedkar's theoretical proposals: How can a generic concept or a generic name repeat a historically particular signifier without itself becoming particular? How can "Christian" be both historically particular and generically unforeseen in its newness? Isn't the explanation of a particular religion with a sociological and theological influence in colonial history promising "happiness' upon conversion to be taken seriously?[14] Of course it is to be taken seriously and in the period between 1935 and 1956, Ambedkar's search for "happiness" led him to religions (including Christianity) for their theological, political, even their aesthetic promise. However this available purchase on cultural-historical terrain should not prevent us from going back and paying attention to the "away" of "away from the Hindus" or "away from their locality". It seems to me that the ultimate aim of "getting away", which I have called "a zero-degree localization", also has a crucial subjective side. The subjective aim is the Untouchable accomplishing a state of radical disinterest in Hinduism. It is not enough to engage with its evils and anathemas; one must push the logic of anathema to its conclusion, which is to produce a subjective rupture with the inherited "Hindu" situation.[15] Ambedkar does not flinch from asserting the "negative" demand in many a delicate historical situation (the temple entry question of the 1930s. for e.g.) that the Untouchables, as a class, do not play the game—which is also to not submit to a destinal blackmail—of identifying their rights with their "corrected" status within Hinduism. Not play into the axiom of "belonging", for better or for worse, to Hinduism, which effectively means to the *closure of a name.* That is the reason why the Untouchable must subjectively separate from Hinduism, not merely through revolt, (for that too is engagement) but through a withdrawal of interest from the "eros" of the Hindu. That is why D.R. Nagaraj, following Gandhi, must be qualified by the statement that it is not axiomatically necessary or a matter of cultural destiny that the upper-caste "convert" to the same measure, mutually, as the Untouchable (Nagaraj 2010, pp. 22-60). This is the subjective "mutuum"[16] that precisely conserves the speculative value of the so-called "totality" which is Hinduism, in the "heart" of the upper-caste as much as of the Untouchable. Hence the heart is already codified and no conversion beyond the measure of the "mutuum", a conversion that produces dis-interest and 'acedia'[17] in the heart vis-à-vis Hinduism is possible. So no conversion is truly possible, q.e.d! "Christian" in "...call themselves Christians" corresponds to this zero-degree belonging and localization in the form of a particular historical cipher of a generic possibility. "Christian" is a generic particular which only indicates in the situation of the Untouchable—and the situation of Hindu(non)society too— the emergence of a new possibility of "becoming-indiscernible" that is not the tactical attenuation and camouflage of "protective discoloration". "Christian" is a kind of historico-fictive signifier of an event "on its way", to-come. So the question of philosophical logic is, does Christianity stand as a name for an event to come, which will also be, in this emancipatory cascade, a name that is much truer and consummated in the "acts" of conversion? In other words, is conversion an *affair of the name,* is the event *nominalist?*

Body, Being, Thought, Use: Four Reasons Why the Event of the Name is Not Nominalist

a. Why does "protective discoloration" fail as a tactic of indiscernment of the Untouchable? Because, the Hindu runs the Untouchable to earth (Ambedkar's phrase) with the relentless application of the law of caste-name as inflexible "locality". Neither the nominal "Hindu" nor the historical improvisations ("Balmiki", "Adi-dravida", "Chokhamela", etc.) will do—the Hindu wants to touch the *body of the caste-name, he wants to touch the Untouchable* with a desperate epistemic urgency that behoves the obsessive, nay, paranoid lover. What is at stake in physical exclusion of Untouchables to the point of proscription of even their shadows is the "making-present" of the Untouchable's incorporeal locality—the desperate stakes of codifying through the caste-name, all the "virtualities" of the Untouchable's body. In these virtualities lie as much the infinite serviceability of the "shudra" of the *Manu-Smriti* (without resentment) as the habitual degradation of the "antyaja".[18] And precisely to this obsessive and exhaustive suction into presence and discernment by name the Untouchable must oppose an *exclusion* from presence-by-exclusion. Ambedkar says that the method of protective discoloration will not serve the above purpose. But it seems to me Ambedkar also says that the formal appropriation of a historical particular name as a generic possibility ("Christian" for example) is too formal a solution to the problem. Indeed the solution is "conversion" but not understood as merely a nominalist upsurge. "The name matters... that name can make a revolution in the status of the Untouchable ... the name must be the name of a community outside Hinduism and beyond its power... Such a name can be the property of the Untouchables only if they undergo religious conversion. A conversion by change of name within Hinduism is a clandestine conversion which can be of no avail" (Ambedkar 1989b, p. 420). In this citation we see clearly the equally great investments in the decision unto a new name and the *conditions* that will make the name work—or not work. However these conditions are not extra-nominal also. The real struggle of the Untouchable to find a "proper" name ("property of the Untouchables") is to find the proper name of a collectivity whose singular dilemma is how to become indiscernible with respect to the "common name"(caste-name) that localizes this collectivity. So the proper name must have the negative advantage of rendering the Untouchable indiscernible to the Hindu and the positive content of being the affirmation of this very indiscernability and singular collectivity. It is pertaining to this struggle and dilemma that Ambedkar's theory of names must be rejoined to his proposals on liberatory "kinships".

b. Earlier in the essay, Ambedkar distinguishes between kinship and citizenship. The latter seems to have a more stable, even static, definition: All it involves is an allegiance to the state and one might speculate, to a "name". This name will admittedly enjoy a kind of "national" content that must compensate for its thinness with a political intensity that invests such nomination/avowal of name conjuncturally. "Kinship" is more complex because it involves the binding of bodies that forms community and the simultaneous transmission of kinship-names through the capillaries of this 'bound' and "networked" bodies. "Kinship" then is both a real entanglement and a formal schema. And, Ambedkar shows that its complexity is a function of historical evolution (Ibid., p. 416). The fascinating interest of all these definitions and proposals is that Ambedkar's essay is oriented to ways of *escaping* bonds of kinship, and modes of dissolution of communal bodies. This orientation is only possible for the thinker "without destiny", which includes the destiny of anthropological theories. Beyond these theories, Ambedkar asks for a theory of kinship with "others" which clearly requires the ontological awareness of two orders of otherness: One, the encounter that makes the other "come-into-existence"; and the otherness that hollows out a portion of existence from the assured continuum of a self in the mode of a ruptural event. But the main point is, both orders affect bodies and their entanglement. An encounter mobilizes and metamorphosises bodies; while the ruptural event produces *a* body, a peculiar one which is hollow and intensely shimmering at the same time. Everything that Ambedkar proposes towards kinship with "others" concerns both a new mode of "entanglement" (or congregation) between the Stranger, who is relentlessly "away" and strangers who are ceaselessly "on their way", and a zero-degree body, a hollow of no discernible corporeal properties. I will not deny that Ambedkar's writings resist the mark and shimmering of the hollow, that necessarily accompanies the zero-point of decision to convert, and in a way enthuses (a kind of logical enthusiasm!) over the new anthropological scenario of originals and converts congregating, inter-dining, inter-marrying, upon conversion. Such a mark (of the hollow) paradoxically ruins (a bit...) the perfect indiscernibility of a "new situation". And yet in the epic passion of his own search for the religion to convert to, Ambedkar seems to repeatedly revisit the "scene" of the hollow wherein the "away" and the "on its way", the decision "not to die a Hindu" and the decision to *live a new life* communicate palpably but *anonymously*.[19] In simple words, Ambedkar knows that there is a name to be rejected, a name to be converted to, adopted and avowed—but there is no name of the event of this conversion.

c. Undoubtedly despite his keen ontological sense of the inscrutability of decision, Ambedkar resists its "philosophy" (in favour of a philosophy of a rational religion, which we will come to) because he does not want the real collective and public movement of conversion by thousands of Untouchables to appear merely subjective, contingent, even if worthy in intention not worthy of *thought*. He does not want the deafening mouthpieces of history to keep reciting to later generations the condescending verdict of understandable, even justifiable, thoughtlessness of the movement of conversion. He wants to give it an affirmative thought-content and indeed the name is the primary vehicle of this effort. Towards the end of his life in 1956 such a name will have indeed been also *incorporated*—a Dalit-Buddhist history will have taken off.[20] But at the time of "Away from the Hindus", things are somewhat "airy" (in Ambedkar's words[21]) and the time of theoretical abstraction is also a time of *waiting*. And it is during the time of this other Shakespearean passion (Ambedkar's, Hamlet's, why not!), that an abstract thinkable form of commensuration between ontology and religion might be presented.

In 1956, with the *Buddha and His Dhamma* it is not unreasonable to claim a fusion of ontology, Buddhist theology and collective politics. Though I must say the picture is vindicated only when we add to the fusion the *act* of fusion itself which is Ambedkar's "Bible of Buddhism". I will go to the extent of saying that this act is the precipitation of a new *letter* of collective politics—what we can call today the politics of Dalit literacy as the creation of a body/letter of being against the caste-name of a pseudo-being. But in "Away from the Hindus" the separation of theology and politics is stark. There is no religious ontology in Ambedkar. Religion is the *considered* application of certain key ontological prescriptions. These prescriptions are egalitarian and *anonymously* universal. All talk of secular "enlightened", "liberal-European" universalism is going in the wrong direction. The theory is that religion brings the institution of a name to these anonymous prescriptions. So the question is: which are the religions compatible with these prescriptions? The important thing here is not to give an empirically specific answer "in

Ambedkar's case" but to state the striking hierarchy between the primacy of the ontological prescription and the *partisan result* that a certain religion fits/follows the prescription(s) most adequately. Thus there is no religious equality, so to speak because equality is not a matter of institutions; it is a matter of being.

Now it would not be out of order for someone to point out that Ambedkar seems to base his "fundamental" equality on some sort of an anthropological duality of people who value "life" as the vital terrain of equal and shared existence and those who don't. Isn't that an anthropologically guided "substantive" ontology rather than a generic one? Isn't Ambedkar looking for a kind of vitalist kinship that some religions institute and which comes as a formal substitute for bonds of blood? But a careful reading shows that even the life-value parameter is only a "primitive" anthropological one; what really is operative in the "modern" cusp of the Untouchable's decision to convert is the *rational* criterion by which the institution of religion will encode and consolidate the *subjective* obligation ("the duty of the perfect obligation") as a nodal movement of communal existence.[22] The Untouchable must convert to that religion which will grant her *the right to be obliged* to participate in a kinship whose analogical schemas might be blood and life but whose updated thinkable content is the pure form of the duty itself. This is clearly the blueprint of a Ambedkarite Kantianism except for the fact that Ambedkar never ceases to re-insert the "airy" formalities of theory into the material milieu of physical as well as incorporeal and spiritual "use".

d. The religious name to which the Untouchable will convert "nominally" pre-exists the ontological—and incorporeal-material—rupture of decision but it is only the decision which makes the name *manifest,* in that sense, creates it. To be manifest is the gift of existence that an event makes to the name. My concluding thesis in this paper is that the manifest name to which an Untouchable will have converted irrevocably bears the singularity of the conversion, which itself is anonymous. The anonymous singularity, however is not a negative perpetuity, something dark and lacking like a spectre from the Dalit's untouchable past; it is the power of affirming a potentiality of the name which then will have made a particular religious name—"Christian", "Buddhist", etc.—into a generic, or in Ambedkar's words, "universal" institution. But because this generic/universal potentiality is the post-decisional/conversional life of the *decision itself,* the institution it inaugurates is an *anonymous* one. Religion, which is the partisan result of a rigorous and passionate collective investigation into the "milieu" of history from which a "religious" name to convert to must be extracted, is the "neo-institution" of a name, or the institution of a neo-name. A neo-name is not an unknown new name one invents; it is the unknown *in* the known names, the new *in* the historical roster of names one extracts as a a generic particular "neo-name".

However the creative affirmation of the neo-name is not isolated from the "uses" of that name in multiple contexts—which are not monotonously religious. The "uses" of a religious name also keep the political, the social and even the aesthetic contexts inseperate from the "milieu" of religion understood as a double institution: the institution of nominative and normative declarations (from the name to the "duty of perfect obligation") and the institution of a "popular" singularity whose proper name is something like a *generic anonym.*[23] This coinage is forcing Ambedkar's elegant theory of names into the cipher of the event of conversion. It is an outrage inspired by Ambedkar himself, and Alain Badiou's appropriation of Paul Cohen's mathematical theorems, including the "forcing theorem". These themes are too vast and exact to be taken up here. And unlike the ideas, the names of references can be dispensed with for the moment. It seems to me that Ambedkar teaches us with his elegant and "airy" pedagogy of the name in "Away from the

Hindus" how conversion is the use of names that is neither nominalist nor hermeneutic. To end on a polemical and negative note, Ambedkar's so-called pragmatism was not a nominalism and his thoughts on religion did not indulge in the mediocre pieties of hermeneutic philosophies—and philologies—of tradition. But to end like this is all right and in the spirit of things because after all Ambedkar's theoretical and 'airy' discourse was nothing if not an urgent demand of liberation from the most polemical, negative and *true* exigency that could present itself—the exigency of the name "Untouchable". A name which unfortunately— and mercifully—Shakespeare will not have smelt...

NOTES

1. For the pioneering focus on the Mahar movement as *formative of* and not *function of* Ambedkar's public philosophy, see Zelliot (2013).
2. Zelliot quotes here from the 1935 Yeola Conference resolution on the possibility of "another society in Hindustan". In an essential sense Ambedkar's theoretical quest is to find the lineaments of a structure of emancipatory thinking that serves the question, which is also a motto: "Is another society in Hindustan possible?" Paradoxically the quest as much involves the de-constitution of all those structural features that are taken for granted in the speculative constitution of a "Hindustan". The Hindus, then, like the other two estates in pre-1789 French Society, are *dispensable* in constructing the new idea of the 'Hindustan-world'(Ibid.).
3. That is why in the larger scheme of things, Ambedkar's relatively compressed, almost rarefied, (we will talk of his adjective "airy") theoretical essay is always accompanied by 'historical' writings of a freer amplitude which throw up "examples" of conversion unmoored from any necessary theoretical anchor (see Ambedkar 1989b, pp. 426-444).
4. We could, metaphorically perhaps, speak of "milieu" as an *ethological* idea in the image of "thought" as an "animal" which adapts, camouflages, metamorphoses—and collapses—in interaction with an "environment" which itself is not stable and has a *plastic conduct* in relation to all the "animals" that populate it. The "objectivity" of a form seems to pretend *repose* that is beyond animal restlessness and historico-environmental

plasticity, a repose thus beyond the pressures of a metaphor...

5. For a succinct and vivid account of Ambedkar's speech, the mass participation of the Untouchables in Yeola, Gandhi's role in the temple-entry campaign of that time, his reaction to the Yeola resolution(s) and Ambedkar's own *generalizations* towards a "programme" of future conversion, towards an *oriented* philosophy of religion, see Zelliot (2013, pp. 147-156).
6. I owe this characterization to a remarkable reading of St. Paul by Giorgio Agamben (2005, pp. 22-25).
7. We will offer some speculations of the notion of the Book in Ambedkar towards the end of this essay but it might be pointed out here that in the piece "Buddha or Karl Marx?", Ambedkar indicates the line of his interest: It is not to speculate on the origins of the universe, through religious or social philosophy, but to *reconstruct the world.* The interesting point is that the 'book' which prescribes and charts out the path and programme of this reconstruction is *part of that very reconstruction.* The "book" is a mirror of the world in the world; so a shattering and remaking of the world involves the same processes for the "book"—while reduplicating the same. Is it possible? In the 1950s Ambedkar will suggest that Buddha's way of "acting" was more suitable than Marx's (as well as the French Republican Thinkers') theoretical prescriptions. And he, Ambedkar, was sort of writing the "book" of conduct and disposition for his "moment" which was nevertheless *theoretically consistent.* How to make theory immanent to conduct such that the latter was voluntarily "disposed" to right theory? For the possibility of a new thinking of the "book" (or Book) in this light see the essay by Dr. Babasaheb Ambedkar, "Buddha or Karl Marx?" (Ambedkar, pp. 444-453).
8. "How can they [the Untouchables] end their social isolation? The one and the only way to end their social isolation is for the Untouchables to establish kinship with and get themselves incorporated into another community which is free from the spirit of caste. The answer is quite simple and yet not many will readily accept its validity. The reason is very few people realise the value and significance of kinship"(Ambedkar 1989b, p. 413).
9. Following from anthropological citations from Robertson Smith among others, the figure of the "stranger" is counter-posed to participants in "fellowship" that make a "family" only as an *analogy* with the parental descensional structure. Hence Ambedkar's meaning of "kinship" is not anthropological but "conversional" or occurential/eventative. One

"converts" to a kinship, which is not founded on anthropological primitives— that is why the notion of "stranger" also becomes equivocal because the conversional fellowship is, and must be, a fellowship with *strangers as strangers* (Ibid., p. 417).

10. Ambedkar invokes, with a scepticism whose intensity corresponds to that of the metaphor in question, Gandhi's metaphor that the true gospel of Jesus Christ (or any other "stranger" divinity...) is like the gospel of the "rose" whose fragrance doesn't require the "act" of conversion to spread... (see Ambedkar 1991).
11. It seems to me that the extremely urgent writing of a "history of the senses" that composes and re-composes every time the elements of material occupation, caste, experience and affect to, indeed, yield a "domain" for the constitution of a "Dalit" subject —the vivid example of the 'leather-worker' composed out of "jati, varnâ and migratory mobilities to yield as a domain, comes to mind—might be fruitfully seen as a history "incorporations" of "incorporeal bodies" that caste-names are in the sensorium of the world. I am grateful to Rajarshi Dasgupta for having brought this invaluable point to my notice.
12. I have emphasized this aspect of Ambedkar's emancipatory philosophy, the aspect of contingency, its rigorous analysibility, its indeterminate remainder, the singularity of its historical effects —in the paper, "Ambedkar Contra Aristotle: On a Possible Contention about Who is Capable of Politics". This paper has been presented at several conferences and its Bengali translation by Swati Moitra has been published in the journal *Charchapad*, August, 2013, Kolkata.
13. In a way we could say that Ambedkar never ceases to try to analytically—and ontologically, when the event arises—grip the *subalternity of circumstances* whose real presence escapes the present of history. But that presence is still in the present—and Ambedkar prefers to analyse its exigency rather than evoke, under its guise, "absent" subaltern names of history.
14. In his essay, "Christianizing the Untouchable" (see Note 5), Ambedkar records several key moments of the history of Christianity and Christianization in India. Is the account held together by the "unhappy outcastes"? Surely not theologically because Christian happiness is not of this world and predicated on salvation-history. But the interesting point is how in the history of conversion and so-called Christianization, theology and its dogmas adjust according to the "tactical" evaluation of particular conditions needed to "provide" happiness *in this world.* So the evaluation goes both in the directions of who needs happiness

and who is *capable* of it. So according to the latter (Roberto Nobili's example of the 17th century is mentioned) the Brahmin is more suited to Christianity while the Christian mission must also adjust to the *conditions* of the Brahmins' "happiness". However in the case of the "Untouchable", the question of happiness is fundamental and goes beyond the particular historical conditions which precisely don't allow that question to be raised. Jyotirao Phule understood this as did Ambedkar—in our times Arundhati Roy once said that the "poor" take the question of happiness very seriously. This seems to mean something fundamental, "generic"—irrespective of their difference of signification, the poor and the Untouchable, inseparable from particular historical conditions yet beyond them, raise the question of happiness *unconditionally*. Which religion's evaluation will be equal to this announcement—that seems to be Ambedkar's own evaluative enquiry on conversion of the Untouchable *in this world*.

15. In an essay called "Gandhism" Ambedkar points out that Gandhi, even at his critical best (or worst) treats caste as "anachronism" not "anathema". I have drawn out some philosophical implications of this diagnosis for our times in the paper "Anathema and Anachronism: A Contemporary Utilization of Ambedkar's Critique of Gandhism". It is due to be published in the year 2014 as part of a collection of essays by Sage India.
16. The reason to use this somewhat exotic Latin word from ancient Roman history in this context is that the word "mutuum" expresses mutuality, relationality, even cooperation through the constraint of a *debt-relation*. This relation and its cooperative basis is not in opposition to unilateral capture of one party by another (*nexum*) but in *attenuation* of this capture to sustain a relation of power and dependence over time. In Ambedkar's view, it seems to me, the "mutuum" would indicate the true asymmetry in the tactic of "mutuality" when enforcing the fundamental Hindu "capture"—a capture by 'installments' to extend the debt analogy. In the essay cited in the above note (note 23), D.R. Nagaraj, while definitely sensitive to this asymmetry, is also definitely drawn to the idea of mutuality as an ethos of mutual transformation. It is not only a question of the "parties" to the Hindu social pact, it is as much the mutual historico-spiritual transformation of such figures as Ambedkar and Gandhi, according to Nagaraj. Sensitive yet speculatively sentimental, Nagaraj's approach understandably has great appeal. It still neglects the fact that what Ambedkar calls "Gandhism" imposes a collective debt on Hindu (-Indian) Society which is so attenuated that

it extends from Gandhi's own time to a kind of permanent Indian future. For "nexum" and "mutuum", see Dumezil (1988, pp. 95-112).

17. This is another "strange" word taken from Walter Benjamin's *The Origin of German Tragic Drama*—a strange book, if any! The reason again is to proliferate a certain strangeness in circuits of mutual "belonging" (Benjamin 1998, pp. 155-156).
18. I have acknowledged elsewhere, as I do here, Sibaji Bandopadhya's sharp pointer towards the issue of translation of the *Manu-Smriti* into English. How to translate, for example, the word "anusuya", "without malice", "without resentment", etc.? Here I will risk the speculative equation between the Shudra's infinite serviceability and the post-Taylorist figure of the infinitely flexible "knowledge-worker" in the history of capitalism, so well brought out—among others—by Paolo Virno. I hope to develop this equation in a more concrete way in a separate investigation.
19. It can be seen from widely varied testimonies that each categorical name, including SC/ST, Untouchable, Harijan, even Dalit, is considered a wound of identity that would ideally close up and disappear into the smooth texture of an uninterrupted social body. Yet no one is disingenuous enough to believe that a social body can ever be or have an "absolute", unconditional givenness. The status of "absolute" rather must be granted that moment of "decision" in history when the wound of identity is both avowed and annulled *in the same move*. This is the move of an "anonymous" absolute whose equivocal status yields both relentless identity politics and radical hollowing out of the stakes in social reproduction. In any case even in the most acute memorialization of identity what is involved is the memory of the "incorporation" of the wound itself, of the hollow which voids the givenness of society. In Ambedkar we find as much the enormous suffering of the wound as the revolutionary historical "sense" that the people wounded are already becoming some "other" people, strangers and kins-people of another kind of "body"...
20. The hypothesis here, which needs to be scrupulously and courageously developed, is that Ambedkar's book *The Buddha and His Dhamma* is the creation of a *new body*, a body of the Letter or the Alphabet which encodes partially—with a tremendous quantum of historical indeterminacy remaining—the new collective movement of conversion. But as a Letter, *The Buddha and His Dhamma* incorporates the "intellectuality" of the lower-castes that is also the emerging "element' of emancipatory knowledge before being a revised theology of Buddhism. Ambedkar's well-known statement of intention that he

wanted to write the Bible of Buddhism must be understood as the desire to create a new body of the Letter among a tumultuous emerging congregation of new bodies and forms. Thus the equation: The Bible=The Book=The Body of the Letter=New Mode of Collective Incorporation of Popular/Dalit Intellectuality.

21. "This discussion on conversion may appear to be somewhat airy. It is bound to be so. It cannot become material unless it is known which religion the Untouchables choose to accept" (Ambedkar 1989b, p. 420).
22. I am grateful to Mohinder Singh for having noted the oscillation in my formulation between the Kantian formalism that accompanies a certain communitarianisn and my own partisan favour for a "communal" composition of bodies and milieus. How much does it affect the truth of Ambedkar in my reading? Probably a decisive amount but I must carry out my wager at this stage... For "the duty of perfect obligation" (Ibid., p. 417). It is interesting that Ambedkar's citation from Robertson Smith's account of the Old Testament Fellowship should have a formal-Kantian orientation. This is not the place to dwell on the matter but there is an engaging literature on the Old Testament Commandments of ethical duty perfectly corresponding to "empty" Kantian imperatives.
23. This coinage is *forcing* Ambedkar's elegant theory of names into the cipher of the event of conversion. It is an outrage inspired by Ambedkar himself, and Alain Badiou's appropriation of Paul Cohen's mathematical theorems, including the "forcing theorem". These themes are too vast and exact to be taken up here. And unlike the ideas, the names of references can be dispensed with for the moment.

REFERENCES

Agamben, Giorgio, *The Time that Remains: A Commentary on the Letter to the Romans*, trans. Patricia Dailey (Stanford, California: Stanford University Press, 2005).

Ambedkar, Babasaheb, "Gandhism" in *Writings and Speeches*, Vol. 9, ed. Vasant Moon (Bombay: Education Department, Government of Maharashtra, 1991), pp. 274-298.

Ambedkar, Babasaheb, "Buddha or Karl Marx?" (Ambedkar, pp. 444-453c) in *Writings and Speeches*, Vol. 3, ed. Vasant Moon (Bombay: Education Department, Government of Maharashtra, 1979), pp. 444-453.

Ambedkar, Babasaheb, "Castes in India" and "Annihilation of Caste" in *Writings and Speeches*, Vol. 1, ed. Vasant Moon (Bombay: Education

Department, Government of Maharashtra, 1989a), pp. 5-96.

Ambedkar, Babasaheb, "Away From the Hindus", in *Writings and Speeches,* Vol. 5, ed. Vasant Moon (Bombay: Education Department, Government of Maharashtra, 1989b), pp. 403-421.

Benjamin, Walter, *The Origin of German Tragic Drama,* trans. John Osborne (London and New York: Verso, 1998).

Dumezil, Georges, *Mitra-Varuna: An Essay on Two Indo-European Representations of Sovereignty,* trans., Derek Coltman (New York: Zone Books, 1988).

Nagaraj, D.R., "Self-Purification vs Self-Respect: On the Roots of the Dalit Movement" in his collection, *The Flaming Feet and Other Essays,* (Ranikhet: Permanent Black, 2010), pp. 22-60.

Zelliot, Eleanor, *Ambedkar's World: The Making of Babasaheb and the Dalit Movement* (New Delhi: Navayana, 2013).

7

Politics, Secularism, Religion and the Order of Things

Achia Anzi

Introduction

Secularism since the 19th century stroved to reformulate the relation between religion and politics. Religion was gradually banished from the public sphere, while secularism was pronounced as the neutral zone in which different ideologies exercise their political power. Charles Taylor in *A Secular Age* describes this political shift[1] in modern Western civilization: "whereas the political organization of all pre-modern societies was in some way connected to, based on, guaranteed by some faith in, or adherence to God, or some notion of ultimate reality, the modern Western state is free from this connection." (Taylor 2007, p. 1)

But the shift from a political discourse which is based on religion to a discourse which is free from it, is only part of the secular story. Secularism in fact announces what is political and what is not. It does not only separate religious organizations from public institutions, but neutralizes the ability to speak the language of religion in the political domain. In other words, in a secular society even the agents of religion have to speak a secular dialect.

Religion under the secular regime, experiences what the secularist George Jacob Holyoake named one hundred and fifty years ago "the conspiracy of silence". (Grant & Holyoake 1853, p. 3) While in the mid-19th century the conspiracy of silence was directed towards secularism, the same apparatus is currently used by secularism against religion. But what is the meaning of "religion" and what is the religious element which is missing in, or silenced by, the secular discourse? This question generally exposes religion's Achilles' heel. While secularism introduces itself as a universal phenomenon, or as universality itself, religion always has a given name: Christianity, Islam, Judaism, etc. Furthermore, 19th century secularism established itself precisely on this ground: by viewing religions as a confused assemblage of contradicting ideologies which can be put to rest only through a secular intervention.

Taylor bypasses this problem; by confining his study to modern Western civilization, and by understanding religion through the notion of "fullness". In pre-modern societies the richness of life, its moral and spiritual value, or rather its "fullness", was experienced as something which is "outside of or "beyond" human life". In modern society "this construal is challenged by others which place it (in a wide range of different ways) "within" human life." (Taylor 2007, p. 15)

In this paper, religion will be examined in a rather theoretical and non historical manner. Instead of reading religion "in terms of the distinction transcendent/immanent", I will follow Georges Bataille's theory in regard to ancient religions, and view religion as a quest for lost intimacy. This approach obviously does not encompass the variety of religious experiences and beliefs. It will serve however two purposes: 1) Illustrating a political discourse, inherently religious, which cannot participate in the political discourse defined by the secular regime. In other words, Bataille's conception of religion will demonstrate another political discourse, essentially different from the secular one. 2) Bataille's theory introduces a destructive force of religion which is usually ignored. This element which exists in various religious phenomena renders the relation of religion and politics in a different light.

A new approach to secularism arose in the past two decades and increasingly influencing the current academic discourse. "Self-described post-secular ways of thinking," Aamir R. Mufti claims, "are fast acquiring a sort of orthodox status across the humanistic disciplines in the United States." (Mufti 2013, p. 7) Like in the 19th century, Secularism is once again the centre of a heated debate. While the secular is viewed with criticism by some scholars, others, like Mufti, denounce this new post-secular trend. If, for instance, "anthropologists [previously] have paid scarcely *any* attention to the idea of the secular, although the study of religion has been a central concern of the discipline since the nineteenth century," (Asad 2003, p. 21) Secularism is studied now within its historical, sociological and anthropological context.

By placing secularism in a historical framework, nonetheless, one might overlook the nuts and bolts of the dispute between secularism and religion. If certain "secularism" is denounced by a critical historical analysis, another *secularism-to-be* may prevail. Moreover, if secularism as an ideology is not understood on its own terms, the post-secularist might find himself standing on the same secular ground.

Secularism, in short, should (also) be read on the surface level, not (only) to demonstrate that secularism is in fact not strictly secular or rational or essentially different from religion, but to engage with secularism as such and the secular claim. Therefore, instead of composing a genealogy of secularism, I will explore the 19th century debate between Secularism and Christianity and study the arguments of Holyoake, the person who coined the term Secularism. In the second part of this paper I will discuss Bataille's theory of religion and its political implications. Finally, via Bataille, I intend to suggest another way of viewing the relation between religion and politics.

Secularism versus Christianity and the Conspiracy of Silence

Beginning on January 20, 1853, a series of six public debates between Christianity and Secularism was held at the Royal British Institution, on Cowper Street, London. The topic of the discussions was proposed by Rev. Brewin Grant: "What would be gained by mankind in general, and the working classes in particular, as to this life, by the removal of Christianity, and substituting *Atheism* in its place?" (Grant &

Holyoake 1853, pp. iii-iv) Grant's opponent, the secularist George Jacob Holyoake accepted his proposal enthusiastically. His only objection, i.e. the replacement of the word Atheism with Secularism, became later on the core of the debate.

At the beginning of his speech, Holyoake attempted to clarify the difference between secularism and atheism, but before doing so he addressed a seemingly marginal issue: "the conspiracy of silence" against secularism. (Ibid., p. 3) Secularism of the mid 19th century, like many other marginal ideologies, confronted an impasse. On the one hand, in order to speak and get public attention secularists had to confront Christianity and hence formulize their position through its authority. On the other hand, keeping silence was impossible not only because it was another way of accepting Christianity, but because silence was the very method of Christianity against Secularism.

> There is, however, a misconception common to many who are auditors to-night which needs correction. Because of my willingness to discuss with opponents, it has been assumed that I am bound to meet every person who may challenge my attention." (Ibid., p. 3) Holyoake acknowledges that he has "pleaded with the Clergy to countenance mutual discussion." However he declares: "our resolution respecting discussion has been measured. We will not say, "Discussion is **invited**;" ... because the Clergy assume that we court them, and that we cannot win the public ear without the attraction of their presence. We do not say, "Discussion is **permitted**," because that to some seems to imply a condescension or an **authority** to withhold it. For a similar reason we do not say, "Discussion is **allowed**," because that to others seems to imply that the **right to disallow** it... We therefore state on our announcements **simply**, "The opportunity of discussion is afforded". (Ibid., p. 3 my emphasis)

"The opportunity of discussion," nevertheless, is everything but a simple announcement as Holyoake finally proclaims. It has to bypass the obstacles of invitation, authority and allowance. The debate is the tip of the iceberg in the secret relations of silence and speech. While analysing the domain of utterance, several questions should be raised: Who is inviting and who is invited? What should be spoken and what should be unvoiced?

Prior to clarifying secularism, Holyoake presents a list of non-traditional Christian views which challenge the unified dogma of Christianity: "Various classes of persons are known for their dissent from the popular Christian tenets of the day. Some developed new notions of prophecy; some reject the authority of Miracles, or explain them by the Rationalistic method." (Ibid., pp. 4-5) In addition he questions the traditional Christian position which accepts Biblical miracles but rejects those of the Koran. On the base of these criticisms he purposes "another course" of action which has a "wider application and conveying more instruction. We might bring more into the light those positive truths for which the criticism of the past has been making way." (Ibid., p. 5)

Secularism does not oppose Christianity. It encompasses criticisms arising from Christianity itself. Moreover, secularism, according to Holyoake, is neither a new philosophy nor a new system of thoughts: "We are not system builders; we disclaim the ambition, and we have no pretension to the philosophy necessary for the task." (Ibid.) Secularism holds a unique position. It presents a system without system, a philosophy without philosophy. It is a-system and a-philosophy, neutrality, the ungraspable ground on which humanity exercises its rationality in order to improve its condition. However, in order to establish this neutral ground, secularism has to rid itself of certain elements that occupied the human mind since antiquity. Secularism has to bypass "questions which five thousand years of controversy have not settled; we therefore leave them open to the solution of Intelligence and Time." (Ibid., p. 7)

The secular approach to theology might be summarized as follows: "The world does not want to know more; it knows already much more than it acts out." This approach to politics derives from a necessity. Secularism is not only a neutral ground but the *only* ground to stand on. Since theological and metaphysical questions are unresolveable at this moment, secularism "leave[s] them open... they shall not be with us barriers which shall divide us from our brethren; we will not embarrass human affairs with them." (Ibid.)

The world view is transformed. There is no Secularism versus

Christianity, but a unified position which addresses human affairs and unites brethren in the face of a wild plurality of theological questions. Hence, secularism must separate Morality from Religion, this life from the hereafter, moral duty from religious duty. At this point Holyoake can speak freely about his religious views since the problem of religion is rendered irrelevant: "Some will ask, what do I call myself in a religious point of view? The question is irrelevant in respect to this discussion, but it will save time to answer it." (Ibid., p. 8)

For establishing a neutral ground secularism has to omit religion from the discourse, not only the Christian tenets but the very notion of theology, which is perceived here as "Sectarian prejudice". If in the 19th century secularism suffered from the conspiracy of silence, in the secular regime it is religion which is led into the unspoken. The secular method does not oppose religion but renders it irrelevant for human affairs. By segregating the temporal from the eternal, theological speculations from materialistic concerns, secularism does not present a simple binary that rejects religion but sends it to a silenced sphere.

If secularism and Christianity can maintain such a neutral arena, what are the practical differences between those discourses? Holyoake offers a practical example in his second speech: the Shabath, the day of rest or the festival. "I point this out to show how what we call Secularism clashes with what our friends call Christianity." (Ibid., p. 26) Holyoake quotes from a resolution of Bradford's church in which a certain Mr. James "views with alarm the increasing temptations presented by the public bodies and others... by making the Shabath-day a day of mere pleasure." Holyoake adds in square parentheses "why should it not be a day of pleasure?" The debate about the proper use of Shabath-day derives from the neutrality of that non-working day. While Christians will pursue this interval as a mean for the benefit of the hereafter, secularists will keep this day "healthfully, usefully and instructively." (Ibid.)

Grant, Holyoake's opponent, mainly attacks the sincerity of secularism in his speech. Beneath the ideology that paves the way to a neutral territory he traces the seeds of atheism and fidelity. His arguments regarding the role of religion in politics are similar to those that Taylor describes in the introduction to his book *A Secular Age*. The role of religion in the public sphere is to provide a moral and spiritual foundation for the political domain.

However Grant's reply to Holyoake's proposal regarding Sabbath-day follows a different track. His view on this issue can be divided into three parts: 1) Christianity has introduced the idea of Sabbath "against the over grasping of mammon and the eagerness of business." (Ibid., p. 28) 2) While "[t]here are many amongst Christians who object to the opening of such places on Sundays", (Ibid., p. 27) Grant hints that there are still others who might support it and that Christianity as such does not opposes pleasures. 3) Finally he proposes a solution to the problem: "For my part, I should advocate, instead of turning the present Sabbath to a different use, the giving to working men a Secular Sabbath—that is, half-a-day's holiday out of the six days." (Ibid., p. 28) Grant's solution is striking not only because he uses the word "Secular", declares "Secular Sabbath" and admits the limitation of Christianity with regard to the problem of the working men (politics). Grant in fact adopts a secular approach to politics that segregates the eternal from the temporal and the holy from the ordinary. Politics as such stands apart from religion. The Protestant religious view paved the way to a secular logic.

The Order of Religion and the Order of Things

In his book *Theory of Religion* Bataille purposes another way of approaching religion. Religion is not a collection of tenets and beliefs but a way of *being in the world*. Religion is not superfluous to the order of things, nor is it a universality that reorganizes reality, rather it is the very act that constantly destabilizes the order of things.

The "essence" of religion, according to Bataille, "is the search for lost intimacy." (Bataille 1989, p. 5). But since the establishment of the intimate order implies the total destruction of reality, the quest for intimacy can never reach its goal. So long as man exists, the order of things will be maintained. So long as the order of things prevails, the longing for the lost intimacy will haunt it.

Bataille conceptualizes the intimacy of man with the world through the relation of the animal with its surroundings. "When one animal eats another," argues Bataille, "there is no transcendence between the eater and the eaten." (Ibid., p. 17) "We," on the other hand, "distinguish an object from ourselves." (Ibid., p. 18) We do not share the continuity with which the animal establishes its relation with the world. While positing objects, we establish with them a relation of subordination, we subjugate them. The animal, on the other hand, "is in the world like water in water." (Ibid., p. 19)

"[T]he first men were closer than we are to the animal world; they distinguished the animal from themselves perhaps; but not without a feeling of doubt mixed with terror and longing." (Ibid., p. 35) The proximity to the immanent world led to the notion of the sacred. But "the sense of the sacred... is not that of the animal lost in the mists of continuity," (Ibid., p. 35) because man reacts to the immanent order or the sacred with "impotent horror" (Ibid., p. 36). The sacred "attracts and possesses" man and at the same time "appears vertiginously dangerous for that clear and profane world." (Ibid., p. 36) The intimate order undermines the very basics of the order of things. It continually endangers the distinctions of subject/object and the alleged clarity with which we operate in the world.

According to Bataille's formulation, the sacred does not supplement the profane, neither is it a foundation for the secular, nor does it move in a parallel sphere, rather it is the intimacy that continually threatens to break the order of things. From the point of view of religion "the world of things is perceived as a fallen world." (Ibid., p. 41) Man not only subordinates nature while reducing it into an object, but also violates the intimacy that he had with nature and with his own self: "If he places the world in his power, this is to the extent that he forgets that he is himself the world: he denies the world but it is himself that he denies." (Ibid.)

Sacrifice

How do we overcome the order of things? How does religion recover that lost intimacy? While a complete return of intimacy is not feasible, the *sacrifice* draws man closer to the intimate order. "The first fruits of the harvest or a head of livestock are sacrificed in order to remove the plant and the animal, together with the farmer and the stock raiser, from the world of things." (Ibid., p. 43) Sacrifice for Bataille is a destruction but not annihilation. Sacrifice intends to destroy the thingness of the thing. "It draws the victim out of the world of utility and restores it to that of unintelligible caprice." (Ibid., p. 43) The violence of the sacrifice restores the intimacy between the one who sacrifices and the victim, man and the world.

However, the sacrifice-practice is not risk-free. The intimate order does not only threaten the order of things but also the humanity of man. "[I]f man surrendered unreservedly to immanence, he would fall short of humanity." (Ibid., p. 53) Man cannot be human without reducing the world and himself to being a thing and on the other hand, he cannot escape "the limits of things without returning to animal slumber." The festival, according to Bataille, presents a "limited solution" to this problem. In the festival "there is an aspiration for destruction that break out... but there is a conservative prudence that regulates and limits it." (Ibid., p. 54) The festival is "confined to the limits of a reality of which it is the negation." (Ibid.)

The festival embodied a twofold contradicting movement: letting loose and preserving. On the one hand it undermines the order of things, but at the same time preserves it. Bataille's festival differs from Holyoake's secularist Sabbath and Grant's Day of the Lord. The secularist Sabbath that Holyoake invokes is motivated by his political stand, i.e. socialism. In a similar manner to Bataille, Holyoake calls for an interruption of the production in order to preserve social values, but Bataille's festival questions the very foundation of the order of things. Religion does not only strive to liberate the worker from being posited as an object, from being treated as a resource among resources of the industrial order. The festival, according to Bataille, is the very event in which not only the workers are liberated from being treated as an object but all the things in the order of things. The festival is not superfluous to the profane world but it is the very movement that breaks it loose (and simultaneously preserves it).

Religious Politics: Politics of the Unknown

The positing of objects as objects has numerous implications. Object implies objective. Like a tool it also serves a purpose. The segregation of subject and object, the break of the continuity of the intimate order, enslaves the thing, subjugates the object to the subject. While separating the object from the subject, man, in chorus, loads the object with meaning, a meaning which draws things closer to us. But this is, according to Bataille, a self-deception. Object might be "the subject's property, the subject's thing, but is nonetheless impervious to the subject." (Ibid., p. 29)

The positing of an object as such is an assault on the object. Only after tearing the thing from the continuity of the immanent order—which in its essence "serve no purpose, has nothing to do, and means nothing"—man is able to force meaning and attach proximity to the object. Only the immanent order has "value in itself, not with a view to something else." (Ibid., p. 29) Our knowledge of objects, tools and manufactured objects is external. They are far from us in the sense that "they remain closed to us", and near us in the sense that we can reproduce them. However, man might be able to reproduce any given object but is unable to reproduce himself. "I would not be able to make another being like me in the way that a watchmaker makes a watch... and as a matter of fact I don't know what the being is that I am, nor do I know what the world is and I would not be able to produce another one by any means." (Ibid., p. 30)

The world-view of religion, according to my reading of Bataille, rotates around this mast. Religion does not operate with a sense of knowing enough to act as Holyoake puts it, but acts with a sense of not really knowing. Religious politics, or politics from the point of view of religion, admits that there is a wider sphere it cannot grasp or understand, and that the world surrounding us and the men inside it are shrouded with mystery. Religion does not try to establish the right order of things, the proper political course of action. Its aim, in fact, is the contrary. It strives to undermine the order of things and bring men closer to the intimate order.

Accordingly, Bataille does not view the military order and the industrial growth (or alternatively fascism and capitalism) from the point of view of morality but from the perspective of the intimate order. While the intimate order is violent and destructive, it differs from the violence of the military order. The violence of the sacrifice and the festival are directed inward and not outward as military violence. The aim of the military order is to expand the empire and as such it fortifies the order of things. "Armed action destroys others or the wealth of others." (Ibid., p. 57) In that sense, through this violence, "the enemy is not treated as a thing". (Ibid., p. 58) But the aim of this violence is not to come closer to the lost intimacy. "[T]he warrior reduces his fellow men to servitude. He thus subordinates violence to the most complete reduction of mankind to the order of things. " (Ibid., p. 59)

In a similar manner Bataille analyses the capitalist and post-capitalist order. In archaic society, production, following the apparatus of the sacrifice, "was subordinated to nonproductive destruction". (Ibid., p. 90) The violence of the intimate order was the "real end" of production. In "the reign of autonomous things... the world of industry," on the other hand "[a]cts ceased to have a subordinate value with regard to rediscovered intimacy".(Ibid., p. 92) The capitalist order marks the complete triumph of the order of things. The quest for lost intimacy "was abandoned by productive mankind". (Ibid.) The capitalist order does not only maintain a distance between man and the world but estranges man from himself.

Epilogue

Bataille's theory of religion is rooted within the phenomenological and the existential schools of thought. In order to fully grasp it, it should be viewed within its proper theoretical climate. The purpose of this paper, however, is not to achieve a better understanding of Bataille's philosophy, but to consider its implications to the question of religion and politics. Instead of advocating one religion or another, or promoting its universality, I proposed to view religion (also) as the apparatus that undermines the order of things. While secularism claims to be the neutral ground on which different ideologies can compete and exercise their political power, religion is the component which constantly undermines, deconstructs and shakes whatever is understood to have acquired a firm ground.

NOTES

1. Taylor discusses two other "modes" of secularity: (1) "the falling off of religious belief and practice, in people turning away from God..." (Taylor 2007, p. 2) and (2) religious belief becomes "one human possibility among others."(Ibid., p. 3) This paper is concerned with the first "sense" of secularity: the absence of religion in public space.

REFERENCES

Asad, Talal, *Formations of the Secular: Christianity, Islam, Modernity* (Stanford: Stanford University Press, 2003).

Bataille, Georges, *Theory of Religion* (New York: Zone Books, 1989).

Grant, Brewin and Holyoake, George Jacob, *Christianity and Secularism: Report of a Public Discussion* (London: Ward and Co., 1853).

Mufti, Aamir R, *Why I Am Not a Postsecularist*, Boundary 2, Spring 2013 (Durham: Duke University Press, 2013).

Taylor, Charles, *A Secular Age* (Cambridge, Massachusetts, London: The Belknap Press of Harvard University Press, 2007).

8

Nagarjuna: The Mystic Dialectician

Dhananjay Singh

Two of the fundamental premises of classical Indian traditions are that there is no closure to any text or statement, and, secondly, an interpretation or commentary is as seminal as the statement it is interpretation of. There is no original statement as much as the concept of linear time is inadmissible to these thinkers. The so-called first statement or text is a half-statement, revered more for what it leaves unsaid than for what it says. Therefore, it becomes imperative to read the first statement with a commentary that acquires the same status as the text. A text is incomplete without its commentary; in fact it is dependent upon it. Due to the oral mode of composition, transmission, and dissemination of the discourses, the philosophical texts are aphoristic and inscrutable. And it is left to the genius of a commentator, sometimes centuries later, to unfold the true meaning of the text. In fact, in some cases, the commentary occupied more centrality than the text. For example, Abhinavagupta's commentary *Abhinavabhariti* is accorded more importance in the domain of aesthetics than Bharata's *Natyashastra*.

In an oral culture, the presence of a rich repertoire of commentaries has ensured the survival of texts in each domain of knowledge. Every foundational text is subsequently followed by a commentary that interprets as well as extrapolates the statements contained in the original text. "The commentary tradition is a cumulative tradition, i.e. a long line of commentaries on a given text generally follow each other, each succeeding commentary taking into account and building on the preceding one" (Kapoor, p. 49). The first commentary is followed by a series of argumentative commentaries, as scholars emerge in different periods with often oppositional philosophical affiliations and argue about the key philosophical categories contained in the master text from their respective standpoints. The argumentative tradition accords the highest status to that commentator, whose commentary survives the vicissitudes of time by logically refuting all the contentions of the subsequent commentators. This commentary does not bring the original text into closure but unfolds its myriad meanings for the receptors to gauge its philosophical profundity. It is in this context Nagarjuna occupies a central importance in the Buddhist philosophy. Buddha's *Kacciiyanagotta-sutta* is as incomplete without Nagarjuna's *Mulamadhyamakakarika* as Panini's *Ashtadhyayi* is without Patanjali's *Mahabhashya*. Chandrakirti's *Prasannapada* is again a commentary on Nagarjuna's *great* commentary *Mulamadhyamakakarika*.

This paper argues that Nagarjuna's cutting-edge argument in his text is aimed to liberate experience from the clutches of thought and language. This requires the philosopher to perform the dual function of a dialectician as well as a mystic. As a dialectician he breaks human thought in its linguistic as well as non-linguistic form to its bare essentials as well as its various combinations and permutations to render its entire edifice self-contradictory. As a mystic, very much like the Buddha himself, he reveals the possibility of pure experience, the true light of wisdom, of *nirvana* and *shunyata* that can make one *tathagata* (the enlightened one) in this life.

As a dialectician, he contests not only with the non-Buddhist schools of thought such as Nyaya-Vaisheshika and Vedanta, but also the rival Buddhist schools of both Therevada and Mahayana schools. While he refutes the non-Buddhist notions of self, body, nature, existence, non-existence, language, knowledge, cause, effect etc., his primary objectives in the text is to interpret the Buddha's discourse and provide it the strength of logic so as to free it from the sectarian distortions of the Buddha's words by certain Buddhist schools.

He was undoubtedly the most influential philosopher of the Mahayana tradition. David J. Kalupahana calls him "the second Buddha," who "occupied second position in the line of patriarchs in almost all schools of Mahayana Buddhism..." (Kalupahana 2006, p. 2). However, as is characteristic of almost all the thinkers of the classical Indian traditions, biographical accounts about him are inadequate to ascertain his period or place of birth. Ian Mabbett describes the problem of historically ascertaining the identity of the philosopher:

> Nagarjuna, the founder of Madhyamaka, is an enigma. Scholars are unable to agree upon a date for him (within the first three centuries A.D.), or a place (almost anywhere in India), or even the number of Nagarjunas (from one to four). This article suggests that none of the commonly advanced arguments about his date or habitat can be proved; that later Nagarjunas are more likely to have been (in some sense) the authors of pseudepigrapha than real individuals; that the most attractive (though unproved) reading of the evidence sets Nagarjuna in the general area of the Andhra country in about the third century A.D. (Mabbett 1998, p. 332).

Mabbett's claim of placing the time of Nagarjuna in the 3rd century A.D. is based on the archaeological findings of K.R Subramanian published in 1932 as *Buddhist Remains in Andhra.* Noted Nagarjuna scholars such as David Kalupahana also accept Subramanian's findings and places Nagarjuna in between 150 to 250 A.D. (Ibid.).

Nagarjuna's contestations in this text is primarily directed against those sects belonging to the Sthaviravada School such as Sarvastivada and Sautrantika. The commenters of these schools brought a great deal of corruption of the Buddha's discourses compiled in the Nikaya-s and Agama-s. Sarvastivada, for example, promoted a theory of *svabhava* (self-nature) or substance of the objects of existence, while the Sautrantika held *kshanikavada* (a theory of absolute momentariness). Both these theories were contrary to the teachings of the Buddha. It was left to the mystic dialectician Nagarjuna to clear the Buddha's teachings from the corruptions spread by the rival schools. Though his main targets were these Buddhist schools, in refuting their arguments Nagarjuna also refuted the non-Buddhist philosophers. The title of the text itself conveys the rejection of the theory of permanence promoted by the Sarvastivadin-s and that of non-existence preached by the Sautratika-s. *Mulmadhyamakakarika* (*Verses on the Middle Way*) also argues the middle path between the discourse and practice of extreme austerity for *moksha* (liberation) preached by the *astika* schools of the Hindu thought as well as the theory of self-indulgence spread by the Carvaka-s (the Materialists).

In the Vedic and Upanishadic tradition the mystic experience involves the revelation of Brahman, the ultimate reality. Bhartrahari, a 5th century philosopher of Shabda-Advaita, speaks of Brahman as:

> The Brahman who is without beginning or end, whose very essence is the Word, who is the cause of the manifested phonemes, who appears as the objects, from whom the creation of the world proceeds.

The *vrtti* (commentary) of this verse further states:

> It is solemnly declared here that Brahman is beyond all representations; it is endowed with the powers which are neither identical with it nor different from it; it has two aspects, that of unity (*vidya*) and that of diversity (*avidya*)...The Brahman is both effect and cause, it is many and one and in all different systems, the manifestations are not conceived as having nothing before or after them. Nor is any limit admitted, above and below, or sideways, to its spatial differentiation.

("Brahmakanda" verse I *Vakyapadiya*)

Bhartrahari too speaks about the mystic experience as a freedom from the empirical world constituted by *nama-rupa* (names and forms). Does that mean that Nagarjuna's *nirvana* is equivalent to the Advaita's *moksha*, and what he indicates as *shunyata* is similar to Bhartrhari's *sphota* or *para-vaka*?

The most basic clue to the difference between the two philosophies lies in the notion of causality. *Brahman* is a blissful mystic experience of pure consciousness that liberates one from the world of conceptual and linguistic construct. But Brahman as an ultimate reality is understood as the first cause, which also manifests as the world (*maya*) at an empirical level of existence. There is a tendency in this thought to provide an essence to both the ultimate principle as well as the objects of world. Sarvastivada also shares the view that the objects of the world constitute a self-nature. Nagarjuna's contestations focuse on rendering the notion of causality a mere construct of thought and language.

One of earliest utterances on a Brahman as the ultimate cause of the universe is contained in the *Aitareya Upanishad*:

1. Hari OM. In the beginning the Spirit was One and all this (universe) was the Spirit; there was nought else that saw. The Spirit thought, "Lo, I will make worlds from out of my being".
2. These were the worlds he made: *ambhah*, of the etheral waters, *maricich*, of light, *mara* of death and mortal things, *apah*, of the lower waters. Beyond the shining firmament are the ethereal waters and the firmament is their base and resting-place; Space is the world of light; the earth is the world mortal; and below the earth are the lower waters.
3. The Spirit thought, "Lo, these are the worlds, and now will I make me guardians for my worlds" Therefore he gathered the Purusha out of the waters and gave Him shape and substance.
4. Yea, the Spirit brooded over Him and of Him thus brooded over the mouth broke forth, as when an egg is hatched and breaketh ; from the mouth brake speech and of speech fire was born. The nostrils brake forth and from the nostrils Breath and of Breath air was born. The eyes brake forth and from the eyes Sight and of Sight the Sun was born. The ears brake forth and from the ears Hearing and of Hearing the regions were born. The Skin brake forth and from the Skin hairs and from the hairs herbs of healing and all trees and plants were born. The heart broke forth and from the heart Mind and of Mind the moon was born.

The navel broke forth and from the navel *apana* broke forth and of *apana* Death was born.
The organ of pleasure broke forth and from the organ seed and of seed the waters were born.

(*Aitaraya Upanishad*, Chapter I. Section I.)

The seer attributes the ultimate cause to the Spirit who speaks in the voice of a person. This is the philosophy of permanence that bestows absolute identity to the self as well as the objects of the world. All schools of Vedic-upanishadic traditions draw on this notion of causality, where all the objects and events of the universe are related in the chain of cause and effect, which is connected ultimately to the final cause Brahman. Even Samkhya that does not posit Brahman is based on *satkaryavada* (the theory that the effect pre-exists in its cause). Sarvastivada, while it denies the metaphysical doctrine of ultimate cause, puts forth another theory of permanence in its assertion that the all the objects (*sarva*) exist (*asti*).

Nagarjuna would argue that not only the philosophy of ultimate cause or permanence is untenable, but that of non-existence or extreme momentariness is equally difficult to logically defend. The Caravaka-s (the Materialists) refuted the spiritual principle of the Upanishads. They held matter as independent and exclusive reality of the universe. They argue that the matter undergoes change due to the essential nature (*svabhava*) of the objects. Therefore, according to this school nothing exists. The Buddhist school of Sautratika takes this line of thought to its extreme when it argues for radical momentariness.

As a dialectician, Nagarjuna presents the arguments of these schools as rhetorical and then dismantles their premises by the sheer force of his logic. As a mystic, Nagarjuna leads his audience to the message of the middle path preached by the Buddha. The Buddha's middle path is explained by his teaching of dependent origination contained in his *Kaccayanagotta-Sutta.*

Nagarjuna's entire philosophy in this text is a commentary on this short dialogical text of the Buddha. It would be worthwhile to quote this text before proceeding further:

> Thus have I heard: The Blessed one was once living at Savatthi, in the monastery of Anathapindika, inJeta's Grove. At that time the venerable Kaccayana of that clan came to visit *him,* and saluting him, sat down at one side. So seated, he questioned the Exalted one:
> "Sir [people] speak of 'right view, right view.' To what extent is there a right view?"

"This world, Kaccayana, is generally inclined towards two [views]: existence and non-existence. To him who perceives with right wisdom the uprising of the world as it has come to be, the notion of non-existence in the world does not occur. Kaccayana, to him who perceives with right wisdom the ceasing of the world as it has come to be, the notion of existence in the world does not occur. The world, for the most part, Kaccayana, is bound by approach, grasping and inclination. And he who does not follow that approach and grasping, that determination of mind, that inclination and disposition, who does not cling to or adhere to a view: 'This is myself,' who thinks: 'suffering that is subject to arising arises; suffering that is subject to ceasing, ceases,' such a person does not doubt, is not perplexed. Herein, his knowledge is not other dependent.

Thus far, "Kaccayana, there is 'right view.' 'Everything exists,'- this, Kaccayana, is one extreme. 'Everything does not exist,'- this, Kaccayana, is the second extreme. Kaccayana, without approaching either extreme, the Tathagata teaches you a doctrine by the middle.

Dependent upon ignorance arise dispositions; dependent upon dispositions arise consciousness; dependent upon consciousness arises the psychophysical personality; dependent upon the psychophysical personality arise the six senses; dependent upon the six senses arises contact; dependent upon contact arises feeling; dependent upon feeling arises craving; dependent upon craving arises grasping; dependent upon grasping arises becoming; dependent upon becoming arises birth; dependent upon birth arise old age and death, grief, lamentation, suffering, dejection and despair. Thus arises this entire mass of suffering. However, from the utter fading away and ceasing of ignorance, there is ceasing of dispositions; from the ceasing of dispositions, there is ceasing of consciousness; from the ceasing of consciousness, there is ceasing of the psychophysical personality; from the ceasing of the psychophysical personality, there is ceasing of the six senses; from the ceasing of the six senses, there is ceasing of contact; from the ceasing of contact, there is ceasing of feeling; from the ceasing of feeling, there is ceasing of craving; from the ceasing of craving, there is ceasing of grasping;from the ceasing of grasping, there is ceasing of becoming; from the ceasing of becoming, there is ceasing of birth; from the ceasing of birth, there is ceasing of old age and death, grief, lamentation, suffering, dejection and despair. And thus there is the ceasing of this entire mass of suffering. (qtd. Kalupahana 2006, pp. 10-11)

Nagarjuna's utterances on this discourse of the Buddha do not promote a philosophy of negation aimed at the rival schools. It is true that in *Mulamadhyamakakarika*, he offsets the contrary philosophies by presenting a series of refutations against them. However, his ultimate objective is to show the attainment of the bliss of *shunyata* or *nirvana*, which is a very positive experience. His philosophy is about transcending the limits of discourse in order to arrive at the blissful state of *shunyata* or *nirvana*, state beyond intellect and language. In this context, the intention of Nagarjuna is to posit the difference between discourse and experience, and to argue that the true reality is that of spiritual experience outside the contours of discourse and speech. In order to overcome the delimitations of discourse and language, it is essential to refute the categories of intellect. The focus of his philosophy is in exposing the innocence of the conceptual categories by rendering them self-contradictory.

Being a true follower of the Buddha, Nagarjuna finds all concepts and statements, more so the absolutist ones, as heretical. To him all those discourses, as far as they claim to know with any certainty any part of existence, are mere illusions. To claim to know about a human self or the world of nature, the human intelligence, emotions, moral virtue and vice, etc. through intellectual modes and communicated through language, verbal or non-verbal, is self-delusionary. The full implication of Nagarjuna's assertion is that he is even rejecting any possibility of idea and ideology as it would inevitably be first based upon the absolute or permanent identity of self, thing, event or conversely upon absolute difference of one entity from the other. This particular assertion of the philosopher is extremely relevant to political discourses, which seek to gain power by employing the notions of identity and difference. Political ideologies consolidate power by propagating identity or oneness of all thereby to crush differential particularities of existence. On the other hand, they consolidate power by positing absolute non-existence of anything or everything.

In his "Dedicatory Verse" to the Buddha in the *Karika*, Nagarjuna says:

> I salute him, the fully enlightened, the best of speakers, who preached the non-ceasing and the non-arising, the non-annihilation and the non-permanence, the non-identity and the non-difference, the non-appearance and the non-disappearance, the dependent arising, and appeasement of obsessions and the auspicious.
>
> (*Mulamadhyamakakarika*[1] "Dedicatory Verses")

The above verse is the quintessence of the Buddha's message as interpreted by his most able commentator. Reality is relative or "dependent arising." The irreducibility of this pairing subverts any ideological dominance. Neither of these pairs can dominate the other or be silenced or thwarted by it, because each is dependent or dependently arising from the other. Nor do they all converge on any point and constitute a dominant hegemony. This verse represents the crux of Nagarjuna's contestations especially against the Madhyamika schools such as Sarvastivada, whose proponents seek to annihilate a contrary thesis on the basis of a theory closely held as true in absolutist terms.

The enlightenment of the Buddha, according to Nagarjuna, lies in a mystic vision that sees the closures of all metaphysical doctrines. The philosophical scaffold of "dependent arising" gives an extraordinary perception that perceives an experience without turning it into a discourse.

The ultimate theses of Nagarjuna, though they are of provisionary nature, indicate the true implications of self (*puggala*), phenomena (*dhamma*), and non-substantiality of the elements constituting the phenomena, *nirvana* (freedom), and *shunyata* (emptiness).

However, in order to arrive at these theses, he must first settle the themes of dependent arising, cause and effect, and change, as they are fundamentally related to them. Elaborating on these themes, Nagarjuna also discards the metaphysical doctrines that seek to produce rhetorical oppositions to his Madhyamika sect and philosophy. These oppositions are thoroughly contested by the philosopher while dealing with causality and change. The most fundamental doctrines of philosophers opposed to the Madhyamika-s, both Vedic as well as the Buddhists, are that of *svabhava* (self-nature/

substance) and *atman* (self)—the essential nature of objects of the world as well as that of the self.

The first objective of Nagarjuna is to reduce to absurdity the very idea of being in his articulation of the Buddha's key phrase of "dependent arising" (*praticcasamutpada*). In the first *karika* (verse) of the text, he says,

> *Na svato napi parato na dvabhyam napy ahetutah*
> *Utpanna jatu vidyante bhavah kvacana kecana.*
>
> No existents whatsoever are evident anywhere that are arisen from themselves, from another, from both, or from a non-cause. (*MMK* I.1)

Before Nagarjuna, there were four existing theories that posited the notion of being: that of self-causation, external causation, both self-causation and external causation, and non-causation. To these theories the idea of a permanent/eternal or substantial being (self/*atman*) was inevitable, whether they talked about its existence or non-existence, or both, or neither. Such a notion of being was posited both in the Upanishads as well as the rival Buddhist traditions, and the first verse seeks to refute both these traditions on this point. The self (*atman*) in the *Upanishad* was rejected by the Sarvastivada philosophers, but they substituted it with the notion of *svabhava* (self-nature). Nagarjuna contests against both this view. He deploys the term *bhaava* to denote metaphysical existence or being, which he obviously rejects and puts against it the term *bhava* to suggest the experience of becoming felt in the process of arising (*utpada*) and ceasing (*vyaya*).

The idea that Nagarjuna questions by dialectically positing *bhaava* against *bhava*, being against becoming, is the idea of ideologically and rhetorically superimposing being on becoming in order to consolidate an identity of essence (an absolute identity) or that of difference (absolute otherness).

The self never attains completeness, and but is always in the process of becoming. However, the Sarvastivada and the Sautrantika schools ascribe wholeness to being on the basis of an error in the interpretation of the Buddha's statement on the four conditions (of dependent origination). Though the Buddha rejected the four causal theories, he accepted the four conditions as reiterated by Nagarjuna in the following *karika*:

> *Catvarah pratyaya hetusha calambanam anantaram,*
> *tathaivadhipateyam, ca pratyayo nasti panchamah*
>
> There are only four conditions, namely, primary condition, objectively supporting condition, immediately contiguous condition, and dominant condition. A fifth condition does not exist. (*MMK* I:2)

These conditions accepted by the Buddha are involved in process of arising and ceasing (of dependent origination), but cannot be understood as providing any sort of substantiality to being. By saying that "a fifth condition does not arise" Nagarjuna is arguing that conditions of experiential existence cannot be distorted to promote another condition, an a priori condition of being. In other words, conditions and being are antithetical, the former being the provisional conditions of experience while the latter being a metaphysical entity. This ideological co-option of the Buddha's message to articulate a sectarian ideology is suggested in the following *karika*:

> *Na hi svabhavo bhavanam pratyayadishu vidyate,*
> *avidyamane svabhave parabhavo na vidyate.*
>
> The self-nature of existents is not evident in the conditions, etc. In the absence of self-nature, other-nature too is not evident. (*MMK* 1:3)

Nagarjuna here firmly rejects Sarvastivada's corruption of what the Buddha indicated by "conditions". What he argues is that on the basis of conditions, one cannot posit the notion of identity or difference. The conditions are acceptable only in the sense that they are involved in the causal relations of dependent origination, but this causal relation is a relation in which the cause and the effect are not understood as having any *svabhava* (self-nature or substance). Following this argument, that denies identity, difference is also denied, in the second part of the verse where he says, "in the absence of self-nature, other-nature too is not evident." What is important to consider here is that he is using the phrase *navidyate* (not evident), hence suggesting that denial is an empirical experience. Getting back to the argument, what Nagarjuna asserts is that if a causal relation can be had without putting forth a unique self or substance, and if this casual relation can produce the empirical identity (not the absolute identity), there is no need to posit absolute difference or otherness (*parabhava*). However, what is to consider here is that Nagarjuna is not completely rejecting the possibility of thought because that would leave experience impossible, but the thought that he accepts is a provisional thought that is a result of dependent origination. He therefore also uses the word *artha* in the sense of fruit for the *effect*, and says that it neither pre-exists as a substance nor is absolutely different.

It is to protect the freedom of experience that Nagarjuna throughout negates the concepts that could turn experience into an ideology, concepts such as time and temporality and the various elements of subjectivity and absolute objectivity (giving nature to objects). He takes up the category of *indriya*-s (faculties) first, as he is interested in experience and the knowledge of experience. He takes the function of seeing (*darshana*), and questions the metaphysical theories prevalent since the time of the *Upanishads*, that seeing does not merely mean seeing the object but also involves seeing itself or consciousness of the self-independent of experience, what Nagarjuna calls "someone without something" (*Mulamadhya-maka Karika* IX.5).

The metaphysicians cannot posit a priori self or personality as an action or an agent of an action is only empirically known. They are not substantial. Those who believe in the permanent self can do so only by considering it as an outcome of the existence of personality prior to the experience of seeing, hearing, feeling etc., which is as unreal as an sky-flower. Nagarjuna in commenting on the non-substantiality of the self in Chapter IX of the *Karika* is elaborating on what the Buddha said in the *Sutta-nipaata*:

> Let him destroy the entire root of obsession, [namely], the belief] "I think, [therefore] I am" (*mantaaasmiti*). (qtd. Kalupahana 2006, p. 43)

Modern Nagarjuna scholars such as David J. Kalupahana interpret both the Buddha and Nagarjuna rejecting the Cartesian theory of self as self-evident. The Buddhist metaphysicians of the rival schools and as well as non-Buddhist philosophers like of the Samkhya system pre-empting Descartes postulate a definite entity as self that is a prerequisite for the perceptive acts of seeing, hearing, etc.:

> This indeed is an unequivocal rejection of the "cogito ergo sum" (*mantaaasmi*) which contributed to the substantialist thought of the *Upanishads* as well as later Indian thought. Nagarjuna's arguments show how self-destructive such an assertion is. The implication of this assertion, as Nagarjuna perceives, is that such a personality has to be separated from the experiences that emerge subsequently. Nagarjuna wants to know how such a personality could be made known (*parjnapyate*) independent of such experiences (IX.3) thus implying that the *sum* is dependent. If these experiences can be separated from the personality, it follows that they could occur even without such a personality (IX.4).

Nagarjuna's understanding of self itself is therefore that of dependent origination. As the external occurrences in the world of objects and events are "dependently arisen" phenomena so is the internal life of a human person the "dispositionally conditioned" phenomena, a result of human deliberation and action.

However, this assertion of Nagarjuna that there is only a self-in-process could raise a moral paradox. A refutation of the substantial being may establish no relation of the deed performed by this person to him. An understanding of the external and the internal phenomena as dependently originating or entirely based in the flow of experience can absolve the self-in-process of moral responsibility. In order to avoid this paradox, Nagarjuna posits the concepts of action and agent (Karana-Karaka). He negates the theories of annihilation of the Materialists and the Momentariness of the Sarvastivada. The former argues that the human self is non-existent, while according to the latter the reality the doer who performed the deed no longer remains. Both theories therefore render the person unanswerable to his conduct making him morally irresponsible.

The concepts of agent and action renders the subject-in-process responsible for the act committed without providing any substantiality to either the subject as an agent and his/her action. In order to counter the Materialists and the philosophers of the Sarvastivada School, Nagarjuna interprets Buddha's message in *Acela-kassapa-sutta* of *Samyutta-Nikaya* as pertaining to the relationship between one's conduct and the consequence. He is aware that this discourse could be misinterpreted as suggesting an idea of self and the other. Therefore, Nagarjuna admits that the relationship between the conduct and its effect or consequence is that of dependence so that the doer is conscious of his moral responsibility. It is not to attribute a certainty to his existence or non-existence or to his agency or action.

In Chapter XII of the text, Nagarjuna reiterates the crux of the Buddha's discourse with his disciple Kassapa about suffering and its cause. The Buddha avoids giving a direct answer rather than refuting the causal relation between the act and its consequence. Similarly, Nagarjuna remains non-committal:

> *Svayam krtam para-krtam dvabhyam krtam ahetukam,*
> *Dukham ity eka icchanti tac ca karyam nayujyate.*

> Some assume that suffering is self-caused, caused by another, caused by both or without a cause. [Suffering as] such an effect is indeed not appropriate. (*MMK* XII:1)

If suffering were to be considered "self-caused", one would accede to the Upanishadic concept of the permanence of the self, whereas if it were to be called "caused by another", the Materialists' concept of the annihilation of the self will have to be accepted. Nagarjuna does not out rightly reject these possibilities even as he is against discursive closures. He denies both these possibilities in an indirect way by calling them "not appropriate," because while he indicates the culpability of the doer, he opposes the fixed notions of self and other, the agent and the action. For Nagarjuna both self as well as no-self could amount to escaping moral responsibility for an act. Therefore, there has to be a relationship of dependence between the act and its consequence.

What is the nature of this dependence? This dependence in general terms in the Madhyamika philosophy is an experience not available to discourse or language, but to be experienced as real. It is to unravel this paradox that Nagarjuna produces his most popular coinage "shunyata". Shunyata does not mean emptiness in the literal sense. It does not mean not having any views or negation of all empirical reality or linguistic construct. It implies holding provisionary views with twin objectives. It is first to unsettle the fixed notions and concepts, and second to overcome the provisionary views themselves that are related to *nirvana* or *shunyata* as scaffold is related to a building under construction.

The Buddha or his commentator Nagarjuna find logically contradictory the absolute distinction between truth and error maintained in the Vedic tradition. What the Vedic tradition understands by error, Nagarjuna calls a world created by language and discourse. But again it is not by absolute rejection of it that the *tathagat* (the enlightened one) attains *nirvana*. On the contrary, it is by appeasing the discursive inclinations that are a result of desires for objects that one reveals to himself or herself the confusion they create.

Nirvana or *shunyata* is a state of pure experience, a free flowing experience. It is a state when the person no longer feels the inclination to form views. But it can be had only by seeing through language and discourse rather than rejecting it out rightly. Nagarjuna understands such spiritual experience is possible through the deployment of language. *Nirvana* does signify freedom, *shunyata* does signify emptiness. However, the spiritual experience involves not clinging to their concepts, but to experience pure consciousness beyond any conceptuali-zation or communication of this experience. Nagarjuna says in Chapter XIII of the text:

> *Shunyata sarva-drshtinam prokta nihsaranam jinaih*
> *Yesham tu shunyata-drshtis tan asadhyan babhasire*
>
> The Victorious Ones announced that emptiness is the relinquishing of all views. Those who are possessed of the view of emptiness are said to be incorrigible. (*MMK* XIII.8)

The ideas of *bhava* (existent), *abhava* (non-existent), *atman* (self) and *svabhava* (self-nature) are creations of discourse, and are results of our inclinations formed in our empirical experience. It is by adopting the notion of *shunyata* (emptiness) that we can get rid of our inclinations as well as these discursive notions. However, it is also important to keep off the linguistic constructiveness of the term *shunyata* (emptiness) itself:

> The conception of "emptiness" or non-substantiality is intended to eliminate the belief in substance and attribute conceived in a metaphysical sense. However, if "emptiness" itself were to be used in an attributive sense that is as a characteristic of something substantial then "emptiness" itself becomes "something" (*kimcana*). A substantial thing is a "non-empty something" (*ashunyamakimcit*). Such a thing does not exist. If so there cannot be something called "empty" (*shunyamitikimcana).* (*MMK* XIII.7)

NOTE

1. Henceforth, *Mulamadhyamakakarika* will be abbreviated as MMK)

REFERENCES

Bhartrhari, *Vakyapadiya,* trans. K.A. Subramania Iyer (Poona: Deccan Postgraduate College and Research Institute, 1965).

Kalupahana, David J., "Introduction" in *Mulamadhyamaka-Karika of Nagarjuna (The Philosophy of the Middle Way)*, trans. David J. Kalupahana (Delhi: Motilal Banarsidass Publishers, 2006).

Kapoor, Kapil, *Text and Interpretation in the Indian Tradition* (New Delhi: D.K. Printworlds (P) Ltd., 2005).

Kena and Other Upanishads, trans. Sri Aurobindo (Pondicherry: Sri Aurobindo Ashram Trust, 2001). Online. www.sriaurobindoashram.org/ashram/sriauro/downloadpdf.php?=33. Accessed on April 15, 2014.

Mabbett, Ian, "The Problem of Historical Nagarjuna" in *Journal of American Oriental Society*, 118. 3 (July-September 1998): 332-346. http://www.jstor.org/stable/606062. Accessed on May 1, 2014.

Nagarjuna, *Mulamadhyamaka-Karika of Nagarjuna (The Philosophy of the Middle Way),* trans. David J. Kalupahana (Delhi: Motilal Banarsidass Publishers, 2006).

9

The Problem of Theatre in St Augustine: Towards a Philosophy of Use

Soumick De

The object of this study is an attempt to construct certain rudimentary but nonetheless viable principles for a theory of use as it find its place within the thought of St Augustine. In order to perform such a task one cannot but take into consideration the relationship of use (*uti*) as a formal conceptual category with that of desire (*appetitus).* It is here that the problem of theatre furnishes a paradigm to examine the nexus between desire and use in Augustine's thinking. But in order to articulate the nature of such a relation, we must from beforehand be cautious not to treat them as isolated categories forced into a relation here but rather as two key formal elements within a discursive terrain which in the last analysis tries to establish the validity of the Pauline declaration: "Now abideth faith, hope, charity, these three; but the greatest of these is charity"(Augustine 2009, p. 28) In this sense love remains at the very heart of this relation which unfolds between use and desire although in a fashion singular to Augustine and quite distinct from Paul[1].

Consent of Desire: The Case of Theatre

In book three of his *Confessions* (Augustine 1992),while talking about this "amazing folly" called theatre, Augustine makes a unique observation. He argues that the experience of theatre—and while talking about theatre he has in mind his own experience of witnessing tragedies in Carthage—transforms misery into an object of pleasure. As a spectator of these sufferings the audience is moved not in pain but in pleasure, or rather as Augustine argues "the pain itself is his pleasure" (Ibid., p. 35). Now pleasure in the form of enjoyment has a special place in Augustine's thought which is inextricably related to his notion of love as craving or desire (*appetitus*). Pleasure as enjoyment in this scheme of thought is nothing but the fulfilment of the desire one experiences. Following this logic in the context of theater, Augustine thus poses the singular question: if in theater pain is offered as an object of pleasure then can misery be the object of love? Of course here the problem becomes even more complicated with the introduction of mercy. Augustine is alive to the fact that to feel compassion for the misery of others is nothing but the Christian virtue of mercy. "When he feels compassion for others it is called mercy" (Ibid., p. 36). But can one compare compassion with a kind of pleasure? Or better can mercy lead to enjoyment? Augustine writes,

> Tears and agonies are therefore objects of love. Certainly everyone wishes to enjoy himself. Is it that while no one wants to be miserable, yet it is agreeable to feel merciful? Mercy cannot exist apart from suffering. Is that the sole reason why agonies are an object of love? This feeling flows from the stream of friendship; but where does it go? Where does it flow to? Why does it run down into the torrent of boiling pitch, the monstrous heats of black desire into which it is transformed? From a heavenly serenity it is altered *by its own consent* into something twisted and distorted. Does this mean mercy is to be rejected? Not in the least. At times therefore sufferings can be proper objects of love (Ibid., p. 36).

But a few lines later he remarks, almost inverting his earlier observation that "some kind of suffering is commendable, but none is lovable" (Ibid., p. 37). What we find here is an apparent contradiction which can only be understood by examining the nature of love as craving in Augustine's relation to the world.

It is Hannah Arendt who first identifies this structure of love as craving or desire in her brilliant dissertation work *Love and St*

Augustine (1996/1929). Arendt argues, it is this expression of love as desire which sets Augustine apart from someone like St Paul in whose thought love also occupies a central place. This structure of love as desire in Augustine signifies a singular mode of human existence which demands that there be an object of love outside the lover who or which, depending upon the circumstances, is none other than his beloved. Thus love as desire always seeks its fulfilment outside the self which loves. This is the terrible isolation of the lover who stands in separation from the object of his love. In order to end this separation or alienation one must find the fulfilment of one's desire and this becomes the true meaning of enjoyment in Augustine. Enjoyment is nothing other than the termination of love in finding its fulfilment. It is the resting place of love where the restlessness of desire finds its peace. "You touched me and I am set on fire to attain the peace which is yours" (Augustine 1992, p. 138) writes Augustine. It is this state of perfect respite, when the lover belongs to the beloved which he calls happiness. Hence there can be no happiness without enjoyment—that is without possessing your object of love. Hence his remark "No one is happy who does not enjoy what he loves. Even those who love things they should not love, think themselves happy not because they love but because they enjoy"[2] (Arendt 1996/1929, p. 19). Because of man's mortality he can enjoy nothing of this world because every object of love in this world is corrupted by man's own impermanence. However this corruptibility does not negate his search for happiness but only distorts it. While what he seeks is outside him, the condition for this search remains caught in the subjective domain of personal happiness. And the final nature of that happiness is immortality. But the impossibility of possessing such happiness forces his personal zeal to be happy —which conditions all his acts of love— to transfer the corruptibility of his own life into the world in the false hope of enduring. Such is the despair of this love of the world which inevitably meets its dissolution. There is then a certain subjective constitution of the world through this desire which Augustine calls *cupiditas*. Thus *cupiditas* is not simply the love of the world which is perishable but more significantly it is the constitution of the world as a perishable thing by the lover of the world who wants to cling on to something more permanent than himself in order to forget his own mortality. Augustine writes "For we call 'world' not only this fabric which God made, heaven and earth....but the inhabitants of the world are also called the 'world'...especially all the lovers of the world are called the world"[3] (Ibid., 15) Against this mundane love which clings to, and by that very gesture constitutes the world which is called *cupiditas*, the right object of love ought to be that which is incorruptible and eternal, that which is not corrupted by the passage of time as is the present moment and is thus projected into an absolute future. In other words, god can only be the true object of enjoyment. This love is what he calls *caritas* "the root of all evil is *cupiditas*, the root of all good is *caritas*"[4] (Ibid., p. 17). It is in this light that one needs to read the contradiction expressed through the example of theatre. Suffering can be an object of love only when it is not to be enjoyed for itself as happens in theatre but when it leads to the true happiness in the enjoyment of god. Suffering which lead to compassion is commendable in the sense that compassion does not seek suffering for its fulfilment but rather the absence of suffering. Compassion is not desire for enjoying suffering but rather an act of *using* suffering without enjoying it, for a greater good. Compassion is thus the love that one feels for one's neighbour who is in pain. But the source of that love always remains god which is the point of reference for all enjoyment. However what happens in theatre is something completely different. Theatre is a place where compassion and mercy which leads to the love of god is transformed into "the monstrous heats of black desire" whose object is no longer the incorruptible and absolute future of a city of god. This unclean desire and "wicked delight" finds its object not only in the pain of others but also in the imaginary joy of lovers on stages which are nothing but mere spectacles. And yet they have the force to transform charity sought through compassion into carnal desire. What is interesting here and perhaps philosophically more important is that this transformation which is nothing but a perversion of the will is not brought by some external presence of an evil nature because for

Augustine "evil does not exist at all" (Augustine 1992, p. 125). The distortion of the will is rather brought about by desire itself. Hence Augustine's profound remark "from a heavenly serenity it is altered by its own consent into something twisted and distorted" (Ibid., p. 36). The desire which should lead to god through an act of transcendence because god is not only the true fulfilment of all craving but it stands inexorably outside the self and the world—that very desire is caught in its own trap by desiring itself rather than eternal permanence. Desire by its own consent folds back onto the world from which it is the only means of escape. While craving should be the means to transcend this world of corruption for an eternal permanence embodied in an absolute future it gets caught in its own mediation. A desire whose object is desire itself is not only unattainable but it moves towards this "unattainability" as its only goal. This impossibility of enjoyment which is embedded within this desire caught in its own immanent mode makes the self disperse into a multitude of things which it seeks successively and yet fails to belong to, moving on to the next and thus forgetting the place of the self itself. Theatre becomes the paradigm for Augustine to expose this problem where the self forgets itself in the multitude of the world. In offering pain as the seeming fulfilment of desire theatre not only tries to create a false sense of transcendence where one forgets oneself for the spectacle unfolding on stage but more dangerously it ensnares desire as an immanent mode of existence which cannot escape into any transcendence and is condemned to play itself over and over like a tragedy. The problem of theatre becomes an example for the enactment of this problem of forgetting the self for the world which he calls *distraction*. The love of theatre is finally a non-sensual love of knowledge brought about by the "lust of the eyes" where one wishes to see that which is contrary to pleasure "not for the sake of suffering pain, but out of a desire to experience and to know"[5] (Arendt 1996/1929, p. 24) his equation of a desire produced in theatre with that of the desire for knowledge—"to search out the hidden works of nature, which are outside ourselves which to know is altogether useless and wherein men lust for nothing but knowledge itself" (Ibid., p.

24)—makes the problem of theatre a veritable problem of knowledge (Ibid.) which will find its implications in the history of Western theatre for centuries to come.

Between *uti* and *frui*

And so one must ask what is the nature of this forgetting of the self brought about by distraction where the self loses itself? The forgetting of the self in the multitude of the world which brings about distraction is nothing but a provisional way of overcoming the fear of death which informs human existence in the world. The fear of death which corrupts every act of love in the world is what true love in the form of *caritas* seeks to overcome. In this sense seeking eternity as the proper object of enjoyment, true love or *caritas* establishes as its goal a life without fear. Fearlessness is the final goal of love which man cannot achieve so long as he is caught in his desire of a life in this world which is informed by change and corruption. What distraction provides is a temporary respite, whereas man needs to truly forget the world for the love of eternal life. In his book *On Christian Doctrine* (2009) Augustine presents us with three categories of things in the world: Things which can be enjoyed, things which can be used and things which can be both enjoyed and used. In this order of things only God is an object which can truly be enjoyed. And if love always seeks enjoyment for its fulfilment then we understand Augustine's following statement "among all these things, then, those only are the true object of enjoyment which we have spoken of as eternal and unchangeable. The rest are for use that we may be able to arrive at the full enjoyment of the former" (Ibid., p. 13) which is practically summed up in the following remark "each man insofar as he is a man should be loved for the sake of God, and God for his own sake" (Ibid., p. 13). Thus everything which cannot be truly enjoyed (*frui*) or possessed must be used (*uti*) for that which can be. This is the fundamental principle of use (*uti*) in Augustine which finds its articulation in several implications. And this principle is inseparable from a certain sense of fearlessness introduced by a true forgetting of the world as we shall examine now.

Through a Glass Darkly: The Question of Transit

Because one cannot truly possess anything for its own sake, to use an object is always informed by an incapacity to possess or won. But in Augustine's thought *use* is not simply defined *via negative* although there is a negative logic to it[6]. To use the world instead of enjoying it is also to use life as another object of this world without falling into the despair of its corruptibility. Since man cannot overcome the reality of death in this life, eternal enjoyment in its actual sense is impossible to realize. But because the singular mode of human existence is determined by desire, he can translate this eternity into an object of desire projected into an absolute future which can be lived in the present moment. This is what Augustine means by *hope* which is not the actual fulfilment of love through possessing eternity but rather the realization of a life without the fear of death actualized through use. *Like looking "through a glass darkly", (Ibid., p. 20) hope clings on to the true object of desire which is outside this world making one free from fear against the despair of the world by using it instead of trying to possess it.* And the only time for this life of free use is the present moment which is rescued from its temporal corruptibility and established as a model from eternity. Since the present is the measure of all time, past and future, it itself as the Now time, stands outside temporality. As a fleeting moment which is always outside time, *nunc stans* is this present instance where as though time stands still. Augustine conceives of the present as a model of eternity standing outside time, where the past as "no more" (*iam non*) and the future as "not yet" (*nondumi)* can meet. This *nunc stans* can be the only realization of an eternity projected in to the future as an object of desire. But "what prevents man from 'living' in the timeless present is life itself which never 'stands still'" (Arendt 1996/1929, p. 16). However in forgetting the world one also forgets the mutability of this self caught in the succession of time. This is what Augustine terms as transit (*transitus*) which is a kind of forgetting that always informs love as craving. Augustine argues that there is always some sort of forgetting involved in love because although the lover begins from a subjective point of view where he has his own happiness as his point of reference soon he cuts himself from this and becomes completely absorbed in the object of love. Thus his whole self becomes "loving". In trying to discover the true place of his self in God, man forgets the place of his self in the world.

The Embodiment of Relation

In desiring an absolute future he gets a point of reference outside the world from which he can now see the world. Thus he renews his vision of the world by forgetting about it. Use is the operation of this new vision of the world in its forgetting. Thus the love of the world, from the regulatory principle of an absolute future becomes secondary or derivative. The "highest good" which the absolute future promises remains the ultimate trans-mundane purpose of a life whose object is still the existing world. There is a certain "'reification' of existence" (Ibid., p. 16) where the transcendental regulator allows life to return to this world as a "thing" among other things to be used for the sake of "the highest good". Use then becomes a form which has as its content this act of forgetting the world of possession. It becomes the expression of a mode of existence which is determined by a fearlessness introduced by hope and which by that same force of logic disregards the modes of possession and the relation thereof which are articulated by law. But this entire process is made possible not by use but by love. Use expresses only a modality of such love. Thus Augustine never fails to remind us that "the fulfilment and end of Scripture is the love of God and our neighbour" (Augustine 2009, p. 25) who is loved *in* use. Thus there is a certain interconnectedness inaugurated in the world where life becomes related to everything else through a new set of relations which is called use. But because such a relation is informed by a certain forgetting of the world what it truly indicates is a relation between the things of the world without difference introduced by possession. This indifference produced by the use of the world where the earlier hierarchies of rights of possession are forgotten in the promise of an absolute future which binds us into a community of hope. "For the sake of" (*propter*) expresses not only the relation into which all of us find ourselves whose reference point remains outside us, it also articulates this new relation as not being dependent upon possession or rights but on a common use which announces a veritable equity in this world. "For the sake of" expresses the interrelationship of all desirable goods such that every desirable good not only expresses itself but the entire network of this interrelationship. Use embodies this entire interconnectedness of the world at its every nodal point. To use something is not to possess that thing but to express this relation. It is an activation of a form of life[7] which has as its content nothing but this relation. To use the world is thus to live in the world where life becomes indistinguishable from the relation it has with the world. And the condition for the possibility of such a life remains a forgetfulness that makes the world a transit which opens it to the arrival of God and the cessation of all relation. Thus to use is to render the laws of this world as understood through rights of possession inoperative. But this new relation of the self to the world actualized by use also places the self in equal distance with the other objects of the world making it indifferent to the world. The mode of existence that use inaugurates is nothing but a pure and simple expression of this new relation to the world rendered through use. If desire was the mode of existence before the realization of *caritas*, then desire is replaced by use with the establishment of hope in an absolute future. Or rather and perhaps more interestingly, as we will try to explain later, in this new mode of existence use does not replace desire but forms a relation with it which Augustine terms "to use with delight" (Ibid., p. 24). In any case the condition of possibility of this new interrelationship of the world remains outside this relation, isolated in an object which is radically removed from this world. Hence God comes as an object to be enjoyed for its own sake. This "for the sake of oneself" makes God completely self-sufficient and hence in a sense a completely alien God. Whatever its consequences might be, it becomes clear that this condition for the possibility of use does not make use an essential category and the ontological level where it continues to function remains at an existential level.

"Love Thy Neighbour as Thyself": The Question of Contingency

When Augustine declares "All men are to be loved equally" (Ibid., p. 19) he has in mind this love rendered through use. The fulfilment of law and the end of commandment finds its expression in this love which always has God as its final and transcendental referent. But To love one's neighbour as oneself is always subordinate to the commandment "thou shall love the lord thy god with all thy heart, with all thy soul and with all thy mind" (Ibid., p. 18). So in the order of love *caritas determines* the love of ourselves and also that of our neighbours. But it is in itself neither the love which we have for ourselves or our neighbours. It is because the final referent of this love is always outside the world, this world can be loved with equity by the actualization of hope which is nothing but to "use the world with delight" (Ibid., p. 24). But who is a neighbour in Augustine? Or better what is the mode of existence for a neighbour? Augustine points out "for the name neighbour is a relative one, and no one can be a neighbour except to a neighbour" (Ibid., p. 21) Thus to be a neighbour is to constitute oneself as a pure relation and express it as such and not a relation between "this" or "that". Hence while talking about the condition of deciding whom to aid Augustine argues that one ought to help whoever happens to be in the neighbour-hood. He writes "but since you cannot do good to all, you are to pay special regard to those who, by the accidents of time or place, or circumstance, are brought into closer connection with you" (Ibid., p. 19). Thus contingency determines the love sought not in the final enjoyment of the object of desire which only rests in God but rather in the joy experienced in the hope of happiness. Augustine while expounding the meaning of the Pauline line "yea brother, let me have joy of thee in the lord" (Philem. 20) argues with a certain existential disposition that although the final realization of this happiness lies only with the lord yet there is an immediate context where to *enjoy* "is used in the sense of 'to use with delight'" (Augustine 2009, p. 24). So we can now place contingency and joy as two key expressive modes which always inform a life of use in the hope of the "highest good".

The Gift of Thought

The last point that we would try to examine is the problem related to abuse which in Augustine takes the juridical articulation of an unlawful use of an object. Now the question arises what constitutes an unlawful use or abuse in Augustine? The problem is not immediately resolved and Augustine does not give a clear answer. But he remarks that if use is the free employment of any means at one's disposal to obtain what one desires, then abuse is related to desiring an improper object. Thus everything outside eternity and the highest good, which is God, becomes an improper object of desire calling for abuse. We have seen before that this is the very form of love which he calls *cupiditas*. However in Augustine we also find the argument that because eternity is that which cannot be lost when possessed it can also be shared with others without itself being diminished. But in this case eternity finds its expression in the gift of thinking which can be truly possessed in its free use without being diminished. Thus when he questions his capacity for interpreting the scriptures he reassures himself through this gift of thought which can be possessed and shared at the same time without corruption. Thus use here is understood as the free use of thought which informs a mode of existence that in spite of being condemned to mutation and finally disintegration can nonetheless acquire a form which opens itself to the infinite domain of thinking as such. The task of thinking is not to possess but to use or better to possess in use something like thinking which always comes as a gift. Augustine writes in this context of thinking "he will give, then, to those who have; that is to say, if they use freely and cheerfully what they have received, he will add to and perfect his gifts" (Ibid., p. 2). Every act of thinking is a gift which cannot be willed into existence. However the condition for the possibility of thought to arrive remains in its "free and cheerful use". One must understand this inflexion in Augustine's thinking where a certain decision to render oneself weak in relation to the world is articulated through his deployment of the concept of use. This making oneself weak is central to them who want to forget this world of possession to which they are tied by fear. "They are no longer to place confidence in themselves but rather to become weak" (Augustine 2008/1991, p. 128) Augustine argues. Thus freedom of the self from the snares of fear and death is to lose oneself in forgetfulness of the world. This becoming weak can only lead to hope which makes thinking possible without distraction but in transit. The transit is not simply forgetting but it is the leap from itself to that which is outside. Such thinking which is not possessed but used does not exhaust itself in being shared. It flourishes in this generic weakness[8] of being used. Such thinking extends itself to infinity so that it can anticipate in its own possibility of free and cheerful use the end of wisdom and the impossibility of thought.

Since every life is consumed in death it is always already an abuse condemned to mutability and the ravages of time. Hence it becomes necessary to transform this abuse into use which too unfolds in this world of temporality yet is always oriented towards eternity. Although it is impossible to realize an actual freedom from the corruptibility of this world one can however become free of the fear of death and corruption through hope and "extend" oneself towards an eternal timelessness. Because use is fundamentally an existential category extended towards this essence it can create a relation between the two. While there is a distinction in Augustine between being as a static and atemporal state and temporality as informed by change and becoming, it is in use that we find a passage where these opposites encounter each other and becoming opens itself to being. This is perhaps the true relation between "for the sake of" (*propter*) and "for its own sake" (*propter se ipsum*) . But in case of "for its own sake" since the thing and the sake for which it exists coincides, this enjoyment also stands outside all human-temporal categories and can only be hinted at *via negativa* through use. Thus use simply opens an impassable passage to enjoyment which cannot be traversed at the level of existence but can only be experienced in joy as a form of life devoted to thinking.

NOTES

1. For Paul love does not unfold as desire to be consumed and hence fulfiled as enjoyment. It is faith rather than love which seeks fulfillment in Paul which is finally consumed in vision. Love rather finds its "bond of perfection" even on earth and is the only way to end mans Godforsakeness. Hence love in Paul remains more important than faith and hope because it is through caritas, that man can find the expression of his attachment to God. Here it is only love which can overcome the human condition which transforms the lover and makes of him a person whose love does not cease in his final happiness when he shall finally attain God in the afterlife. This love continues without cessation in the afterlife as it did on earth. This is a far cry from Augustine for whom love unfolds as desire which will find its fulfilment in the final object of enjoyment in God himself. But as this is not possible as long as man is trapped in his own mortality, this enjoyment which comes as a vision can only be attained in the afterlife when one shall behold the divine and thus consume him in his act of seeing. This enactment can only be that of vision because for Augustine vision remains the perfect form of possession. Unlike Paul for whom vision is the fulfilment of belief in knowledge Augustine expresses vision or the act of beholding as the fulfilment of desire. When seen along Augustine's injunction against theater as the place where knowledge is consumed for the pleasure of knowledge itself, the above distinction resonates with the cautionary tale of a voyeuristic possession of knowledge that Augustine warns us against (Arendt 1996/1929, pp. 31-32).
2. Originally quoted from Augustine's *The City of God* VIII, 8. by Hannah Arendt. It is to be noted that some of the following quotes are not taken from Augustine's original texts but from Arendt's book *Love and St Augustine* (1996/1929). Places where such quotes are used, the citation in the body of the text reads (Arendt 1996/1929) followed by the page number though a separate footnote identifies the original Augustine text and the page number as cited in the Arendt text. Where texts have been quoted from Hannah Arendt's own writing no such footnote has been provided.
3. Originally quoted from Augustine's *Homilies on the First Epistle of John* II, 12.
4. Originally quoted from Augustine's *Commentaries on the Psalms* 90, I, 8.
5. Originally quoted from Augustine's *Confessions* X, 35, 55.
6. In Augustine's thought even when one rejects love as desire as Hannah

Arendt tries to do and establish another way of conceptualizing it through memory and imitation where love is nothing but the actualization of imitation, this other love also maintains a relation to use. Here we need to orient a possible theory of use in Augustine to his larger formalization of imitation as the basic structure of human conduct. Thus to use the world here becomes a mirror image of the divine act. As Augustine argues that God being self-sufficient does not enjoy man but uses him. So does man imitating this divine act which is God himself, uses the world not to enjoy it but the receive God. Again we find a relation emerging between use and love in Augustine, when though from this other perspective, where love in actualizing imitation corresponds to use. Thus to love and to use the world, not from the point of view of desire but that of remembrance also leads to a similar consideration of love finding its expression in use. This articulates a strong theory of use embedded in the concept of love in Augustine which needs to be extracted.

7. The idea of a form of life is inextricably conjoined with the notion of habit in Augustine. Habit for Augustine is only a link in a chain which imprisons man through a distortion of the will which creates passion under whose servitude (evil) habit is formed. And that habit to which no resistance can be offered becomes a necessity. Interestingly this same operational logic of will leading to (good) habit which in its turn becomes necessity can be seen functional in the inverse mode of life which is good and oriented towards happiness. In any case habit which is only a resultant of a perverted will is also the source of evil in the world. In other words evil habit is nothing but a set of actions not determined by any ontological imperative like that of Truth, Good or Equity but those actions which are performed by the distorted will of the soul whose essence nonetheless lies with God. This distortion in the final analysis is forced by something like nothingness which corrupts the actions otherwise performed under some ontological prescription of Good/Truth/Being/God. Since human actions cannot correspond to being because of our temporal existence, our becoming (which is also the realm of human actions) imitates Being/God in modalities which tend to return to this Eternal Being. Nothingness cannot completely absorb life which is impossible before death but it can affect or force the "I" of the will which imitates Being to become "no more I" of a perverted will. This is what habit sustains in life, thereby imprisoning life in the fetters of death. Thus evil does not exist but it can assert enormous power and distort the will to perform evil deeds. In his critique

of the Manichees who believed that evil actions performed by an evil will had some negative substance behind it under whose imperative it did evil as against the good essence which determined good deeds, Augustine argues that there is a certain split of the will existing in the same soul but which can function either under the imperative of the spirit or that of the flesh but in either case they are incomplete. Man cannot have his will completely given to himself, which Augustine calls "wholehearted will", because of his mortality but neither can his will be completely overtaken by nothingness because he has life and hence a will to exist . This for Augustine is the essence of the line from Paul "The flesh lusth against the spirit, and the spirit against the flesh, and these are contrary one to the other" (Gal.v.17). In his book *On Christine Doctrine* (2009/1886-90) Augustine categorically says that this flesh is not to be taken literally as the substance of flesh, i.e the body but "its evil habit" (Ibid., p. 16). Thus whereas there is a certain delight in eternity which makes our body light under the subjugation of the spirit which tries to subdue the flesh (evil habit) and helps it to ascend, the desire of the temporal world holds us down by orienting it towards a nothingness which is expressed in our mortality. The identical soul is torn in the desire between the two and cannot receive wholeheartedly one or the other. Thus Augustine notes, "It is torn apart in a painful condition as long as it prefers the eternal because of its truth but does not discard the temporal because of its familiarity" (Augustine 2008/ 1991, p. 150). From this we can conclude that evil and by the same logic habit, from an ontological point of view, does not appear as a question of essence in Augustine but that of something like existence which needs to be performed or enacted under imperatives which can come from outside as in case of God or from existence itself as in case of nothingness which is always immanent to life as a hollowing out of existence itself (Augustine 1992, pp. 140-141 & 147-150; 2009, pp. 14-17).

8. The problem of the "power of the weakness" in St. Paul is one of the central concerns of Agamben's book *The Time that Remains* (2005). In this book Agamben not only establishes a relation between St Paul's other theme of inoperativity through *hos me* to the point of a generic potentiality of weakness to render all structures of worldly power inoperative (which he demonstrates through a number of sequences unfolding in the history of Western thought. But, further, he makes it a point to rework this idea of weakness (*aestheneia)* through the Greek idea of impotentiality (*adynamia*) which maintains a kind of potentiality.

Citing Aristotle in Metaphysics he writes, "each thing is powerful either through having something or through the privation of the same thing." This is what he claims reverberates through Paul's idea of the messianic power which does not exhaust itself in its *ergon* (activation) but continues to be powerful in its weakness. Here the impotentiality or the potential not to be or not to do, is actualized in weakness (*asthenia*), where it finds its *telos*, not in the form of force or *ergon*, but in its opposite. Agamben brings this problem of inoperativity actualized through weakness down to the Franciscan notion of *usus* or use against right to use. What is perhaps missing from this powerful deployment of the problem of weakness and its relation to use is St Augustine who remains outside his purview.

REFERENCES

Agamben, Giorgio, *The Time that Remains: A Commentary on the Letter to the Romans,* trans. by Patricia Dailey (Stanford: Stanford University Press, 2005).

Arendt, Hannah, *Love and Saint Augustine*, eds. Joanna Vecchiarelli and Judith Chelius Stark, (Chicago & London: The University of Chicago Press, 1996).

Augustine, Saint, *Confessions,* trans. Henry Chadwick (Oxford: Oxford University Press, 1992).

Augustine, Saint, *On Christian Doctrine,* trans. Rev. Professor J.F. Shaw (New York: Dover Publications, 2009).